Leadership, Structures and Accountability in the Public Service
Priorities for the Next Phase of Reform

Leadership, Structures and Accountability in the Public Service

Priorities for the Next Phase of Reform

Carlos Alverez-Antolinez
Derek Brennan
Louise McKenna
Maurice Mullen
Aidan O'Driscoll
Philip O'Reilly
Nacie Rice
Michael Sheridan
Gerry Smyth
Tony Smyth
Noel Usher

First published in 2007
by the Institute of Public Administration
57–61 Lansdowne Road
Dublin 4
Ireland

ISBN 978 1 904541 60 8

British Library cataloguing-in-publication data
A catalogue record for this book is available
from the British Library

Cover design by M & J Graphics, Dublin
Typeset in Garamond 11/12.5 by Carole Lynch, Sligo
Printed by ColourBooks Ltd, Dublin

Contents

Preface

"Public service reform" has been a ubiquitous phrase on the lips of politicians, media commentators and public servants themselves in recent years. Significant changes have been undertaken in many countries, including Ireland, which have affected how the public service is organised, managed and held to account. There remains however a strong view, widely shared, that more needs to be done, and that this is both an urgent and an important task.

The book is based on postgraduate work that we undertook in Trinity College Dublin, and draws on the significant body of Irish and international literature on the subject and on our findings from a research visit to Australia and New Zealand, two countries widely identified as being at the forefront of the reform process. It focuses primarily on the central Civil Service but also makes reference to the wider public service as appropriate. While the views expressed are ours alone, this work is also significantly influenced by our experience in the central civil service and law enforcement agencies in Ireland, and in the European Commission.

Our purpose in writing this book is to make a practical input to the next phase of reforms, which is now being considered. We hope that those reforms will be bold and well-focused, and that the ideas offered here will contribute to those aims.

The group wishes to acknowledge the invaluable insights gleaned from our meetings with colleagues in Ireland, Australia and New Zealand, which were consistently offered in an open and helpful spirit. We are also deeply grateful to all the lecturers and contributors on our course in Trinity College Dublin from whom we learned so much. Most especially, we offer our offer heartfelt thanks to Ruth Maybury, John Murray and John Quilliam of TCD for their unfailing support, advice and assistance over the past two years. We are very grateful to the IPA for publishing this book and for the enormous contribution made by our editors Tony McNamara and Brendan O'Brien.

Carlos Alverez-Antolinez
Derek Brennan
Louise McKenna
Maurice Mullen
Aidan O'Driscoll
Philip O'Reilly
Nacie Rice
Michael Sheridan
Gerry Smyth
Tony Smyth
Noel Usher

1

Introduction

The Strategic Management Initiative/Delivering Better Government programme of reform in the Irish Civil Service has done much to bring about positive change over the past decade. The impact of this is often underestimated.

However, the programme can also be criticised for lacking strategic direction, and was described by one leading commentator as 'spotty' in its application (Schick, 1999). The same author has also observed that in many reforming countries there is a failure to 'systematically evaluate what has been accomplished' and that while most reform initiatives 'typically begin with much fanfare, after a decent interval, most just fade away or are displaced by the next wave of reform'. There is a danger of Ireland's programme following a similar path. In recent times there has been a feeling among civil servants that the programme has lost momentum and direction. Also there is a sense that the potential synergies from all of the individual changes have not yet been achieved.

The Taoiseach and the Secretary to the Government in recent statements have also concluded that significant and useful progress has been made over the past ten years through the SMI/DBG process but that important tasks remain to be tackled. Ireland still lags behind other countries in some key areas of reform. We believe we can usefully look at experience abroad to find pointers for future progress in this country, but that we must be very conscious of the need to base any proposed reforms on the foundations already laid, having particular regard to the history and current experience of our own public service and to the interests of its key stakeholders.

This book reviews Ireland's progress along the path of reform and compares it with other countries following a similar course. We look forward and consider the type of organisations that will be required in the public service over the next ten or fifteen years to meet the rising expectations of citizens and those of the political system. From this perspective we have tried to identify and describe some of the key issues to be tackled in the next phase of Civil Service reform in Ireland while being mindful of the need to consolidate and build upon what has already been achieved. We also suggest some practical ways in which these challenges might be addressed.

Arising from our literature review, from our assessment of the Irish reform programme and from the views of senior Civil Service managers, three key areas emerged in terms of changing demands and rising service expectations: organisational structures, accountability systems, and Civil Service leadership. We explain the reasons for this selection in more detail in the next chapter

We visited Australia and New Zealand[1] for benchmarking and comparative purposes: these countries have among the most advanced modernising public services, particularly in regard to our selected subject areas. In addition, they have similar types of public governance systems to our own, thus enabling relevant comparison. Having been to the forefront in the implementation of the New Public Management reform movement since the 1980s, these administrations have more recently made significant progress in implementing the next phase of reform. On our study tour we met with a range of public bodies in Australia and New Zealand, whose experience with the new reform measures was considered in further workshops, having regard to the potential applicability of these initiatives in the Irish context. Extensive documentary material and numerous interviews presented many examples of successful initiatives and lessons that could be drawn. Conscious of the political, economic and cultural differences between Ireland and the countries visited, we selected material that we considered to be most applicable to the current stage of Irish public sector reform.

---

[1] All 11 authors visited Australia or New Zealand; seven visited both.

The methodology chosen had a number of strengths. In particular, we gained a valuable insight into the thinking behind the various strategies and methods through direct face-to-face discussions with public service leaders in Ireland, Australia and New Zealand. This allowed a much deeper understanding of the issues than would have been possible based on published material alone.

However, the transposition of lessons from foreign experience to the Irish context has some important limitations. In the timeframe available it was not possible to carry out a detailed like-for-like comparison between counterpart agencies in the countries visited or cases reviewed. Our interviews in each of the jurisdictions were with middle and senior managers only. It was not possible to have similar interviews with more junior staff, politicians or other stakeholders.

It must also be acknowledged that information gathered through interviews and published material is often subjective. Given the complexity of the public service and the great variations across jurisdictions, there are few hard metrics that would allow objective quantitative comparisons.

The next phase of Civil Service reform: the drivers for further change

The Civil Service has always been affected by societal change and the evolving demands for public services that go with it. The difference in recent years is the rapid rate of change, and the raised level of citizens' expectation of customer service driven by their experience of new or improved services from private sector exemplars.

The Taoiseach (2006b) underlined the swift pace of change in our society recently when he stated:

> Over the past 10 or 15 years our economy has moved through several gears. Our society is transforming. We are experiencing rapid change to our workplaces, our living spaces and our commuting patterns. We have become more open, more culturally diverse and more outward looking. We are redefining our values – what we want for our children, for our elders and our communities.

The Civil Service, according to Alan Greenspan (2004), cannot stand still or be a passive observer of these changes in society. In contemporary society, adaptation to change is a constant, ongoing process for an institution like the Civil Service, if it is to continue to play an effective role. To quote Haran (2003), 'Securing a culture of systematic and constant improvement in performance … is at the heart of this challenge.'

Haran (2003) identified a number of factors driving change in Ireland. Globalisation is the most powerful and pervasive driver of change, in particular the capacity of factors such as knowledge, people and capital to diffuse globally. This impacts particularly on Ireland, as one of the most open economies in the world.

Continued economic growth in Ireland requires that we put in place the necessary conditions to compete in international markets, and the Civil Service is expected to contribute in a major way to developing an environment that enables Irish businesses to build their domestic base and to compete internationally. This economic imperative is paralleled by the need to adapt to rapid social changes. Principal among these are the growth in the population and changes in the demographic profile, rising educational standards, growing participation by women in the workforce, and the increasingly multicultural nature of society

The quickening pace of technological progress is also driving and supporting the change agenda. Advances in information and communication technology (ICT) over the past decade have seen very significant changes in the delivery of government services, many of which can be easily availed of online. However, the use of the Internet in this way is still relatively new. Its full impact in terms of both providing existing services and creating demand for new services has not yet been felt.

The standard of customer service expected by citizens today is equivalent to that available from the best providers in the private sector. This is true whether or not there is a similar product or service available in the private sector. This increased level of expectation of service requires public services to be as responsive and as flexible as the best private companies operating in the marketplace. Failure to meet these exacting standards will lead to pressure on the political system to deliver, and bring a pressure on the department or agency to change its response. The increased wealth of the country means that the citizens no longer accept lack of available funding as a valid reason for a lack of, or inadequate, service.

Standards of transparency and accountability are also changing. There is a trend in many countries, and especially among the OECD countries, towards more open government as evidenced by legislative changes such as freedom of information (FOI), data protection, and ethics legislation. Following some high-profile financial scandals in the international arena, culminating in the collapse of a number of large multinational corporations, there is also increased concern about corporate governance. This has had ramifications for public sector governance and underpins the demand for open and transparent accountability.

Citizens' increased expectations of service and performance in this environment of constant change, and the requirement to be more open and accountable in the decision-making processes, require that government service organisations constantly examine what they deliver and seek new ways to meet these expectations. The Civil Service must therefore seek constant internal improvement in its operations. As Schick (2003) suggests, reform is not just a matter of strategy and tactics, but also of opportunities and timing. In the light of the drivers and the changes referred to above, service delivery improvement is not a matter of a single step change, but an ongoing process. In such an environment we must create a culture of ongoing improvement, where change is the norm. In the face of these challenges government organisations must, as stated by Haran (2003), be 'nimble and agile' in order to adapt quickly and flexibly to meet emerging needs.

Stakeholder expectations of a modern Civil Service

The next phase of public sector reform must take account of the drivers described in the preceding section. In a society and political process characterised by a strong tradition of consensus and social partnership, it must also be informed by the views of major stakeholders.

Government, politicians and citizens are the key stakeholders in the Civil Service. Others include businesses, trade unions, and social partners. Civil servants themselves are also stakeholders, in that they have a direct interest in their own development and in the professionalism with which public services are delivered. Within this group the trade unions representing the civil and public servants are also recognised as stakeholders.

The political system

Politicians want a Civil Service that is capable of delivering the Government's stated policies. This includes delivering capital projects on time and within budget and providing top-quality front-line services. From the perspective of the politician, significant issues and challenges facing the Civil Service may be grouped under three main headings: (1) service delivery, (2) renewal and transformation, and (3) the public service contribution to national development (An Taoiseach, 2006b).

Service delivery demands the capacity to develop front-line services to citizens that are both responsive and inclusive. It demands the capability for project management, particularly in the delivery of large infrastructural projects. It also calls for the developing complexities of a more culturally and ethnically diverse society to be addressed.

The Taoiseach has highlighted the demand for more and better services, coupled with greater accountability for the performance the Civil Service delivers with taxpayers' money. In an address to the Irish Management Institute (2006c) he stated that 'The Public Service has to earn public confidence in its ability to deliver – the taxpayers expect value for their money' and 'the Public Service needs to demonstrate that it gives value in those areas of service delivery where alternative channels now exist.'

This theme is echoed in a joint document by the Fine Gael and Labour parties (2006), which points out that:

> Inefficient public spending represents a drain on our economy and a threat to our present and future competitiveness. Where public services and productive infrastructure are provided at a cost far greater than the cost of similar provision in other countries, Ireland is at a corresponding competitive disadvantage … the Irish

people have a right to expect world-class public services, efficiently delivered. The Irish taxpayer has a right to value for money.

Renewal and transformation of the public service encompasses the management and the development of staff where new and flexible work patterns are appearing, the need for financial systems to support the application of accountability systems that are more focused on outcomes, and the need to use the opportunities presented by the emerging information and communication technologies to improve the quality and extent of public services available to citizens. The Taoiseach has stated, in an address to the Institute of Public Administration (2006b), that public service organisations must be more flexible and responsive to change and the Civil Service needs to modernise the way it manages human and financial resources. Opposition political parties point out that 'There is insufficient flexibility in the system to divert resources to meet emerging needs, and to ensure that money flows to areas where results are being achieved' (Fine Gael and Labour, 2006).

The public service contribution to national development and economic success is crucial. The role of the public service as 'an enabler of national progress' was underlined by the Taoiseach in a recent address. However, there is a need for continued progress in areas such as quality regulation for both the business sector and citizens, the development of processes to deal with cross-departmental issues, and the implementation of the longer term policy goals of Government.

Politicians of all parties want a Civil Service that possesses the appropriate professional skills at all levels to deliver key programmes. The Taoiseach has acknowledged that Ireland has been well served by its public servants but pointed to noticeable gaps in the skills base, and to a system of recruiting senior managers that is no longer appropriate to modern needs. Politicians want the Civil Service to deliver initiatives and projects on time and in a manner that provides value for money. They want the appropriate structures in place to allow this to happen, and where it is not happening, they want proper accountability systems to allow issues to be identified and addressed.

The business community

The cost of doing business in Ireland impacts on our ability to compete on the international stage. Such costs include those associated with employing staff and complying with the various rules and regulations applying in an advanced economy that places a high value on its social responsibilities and commitments. The business community is also concerned with the cost and convenience of public infrastructure.

The Civil Service plays a key role in the design and implementation of the regulatory framework, which shapes the commercial environment. Finding the right balance between regulation and the operation of a free market, and maintaining a competitive edge in an increasingly globalised world, is crucial to our success. McGinty (2003) acknowledged this when he said that 'Part of any country's competitiveness is the efficiency of the delivery of its public services.'

The ongoing modernisation of the public service is therefore a legitimate concern of the business community, particularly in the areas of public service employment structures and human resources (HR) management. They also see a need for outcome performance appraisal and accountability mechanisms.

Civil Service staff

The expectations of staff for the organisation of the future must be considered. To attract and retain the calibre of staff necessary to deliver the quality of services required by its stakeholders, and to be an employer of choice, the Civil Service must have attractive terms and conditions of employment. People prefer to work where their talents are being used and developed. Some public service employment conditions – such as flexible working hours and family-friendly policies, which allow staff to choose their work/life balance – are already quite attractive for many grades, but as the

competition for talented staff continues, other dimensions of
the total rewards package must be explored.

Trade unions

The public service is one sector of the economy where trade
union membership has remained strong. This gives the trade
union movement a special interest in the reform proposals
for the public services generally and for the Civil Service in
particular. The challenge for Civil Service management in
implementing change is thus compounded by the political
necessity of negotiating with the trade union movement
inside the Partnership process. As a consequence, the national
agreements tend to reflect the unions' view that change and
modernisation in the public services should proceed gradually as part of an agreed productivity and pay process.

The general public

The general public are ultimately the key stakeholder in the
Civil Service. What do the general public want from the Civil
Service? 'In every developed country, people want higher
standards and better customer service, but not higher taxes'
('Meeting the demand for improved public services', 2007).
Thus the first issue for the Civil Service is ensuring delivery
of the types of services that the public wants. The second is
the manner of delivery or customer service quality. Finally
there is the perceived efficiency of delivery and the integrity and impartiality of the delivery mechanism.

The voice of the public is sometimes heard through lobby
groups, but these are typically single-issue organizations
highlighting particular difficulties or shortfalls. To get a
broader balanced view of what the Irish public wants, it is
necessary to look at more comprehensive customer surveys
such as those carried out for the National Development Plan
by Ipsos MORI in March 2006 (Department of the Taoiseach,
2006), which found that the public were generally very
happy with the customer service quality they were getting
from the Irish Civil Service. The two top issues of national

concern were crime and health, followed by traffic conges-
tion and environmental issues. These are areas of service
delivery that the public feel are not fully under control or
where delivery is inadequate.

A high percentage of the public consider the Civil Service
to be efficient but express concerns about getting value for
money in capital spending programmes under the National
Development Plan. While a large majority of the public
believes the Civil Service to be independent and trustworthy,
according to the 2006 survey, the public attaches high
importance to transparency and accountability. Among the
key drivers for generating customer satisfaction are timeli-
ness in delivery, professionalism and customer focus, and
the availability of information and complaints procedures.

Towards 2016

One place where the various stakeholders come together
and form a joint, negotiated view is in the Social Partnership
process. The current agreement – *Towards 2016* – sets out
the framework for public service modernisation and flexibility. This includes agreement to changes in existing structures
and working methods to ensure that services are provided in
the most efficient and effective way. It recognises the need
for co-operation on issues such as team working and cross-
functional working (in place of traditional reporting
relationships), the use of new technology and e-government.
The agreement provides the framework for examining alternative service delivery options, including the employment of
temporary staff, contracting out of work or outsourcing to
the private sector or to other public sector bodies.

For the Civil Service there are additional commitments to
modernisation and change including improvements to the
existing recruitment and promotion systems. This will allow
for expanded use of open recruitment and competitive
merit-based promotion.

Meeting the required standards of performance and delivery

In summary, the Irish Civil Service of the future must be organised in such a way as to deliver the services required by citizens and the political system in an efficient and effective manner. It must be adaptive, flexible, and responsive to meet the changing demands for service, and the exacting standards of performance and accountability expected in a modern society.

To meet the needs of the various stakeholders, the Civil Service needs to become performance-focused – delivering improved everyday front-line services to citizens, anticipating future needs, delivering and implementing systems and procedures to support and underpin political decision-making, and ensuring value for money. Politicians in particular – in their quest for greater responsiveness – want a Civil Service that not only generates ideas and develops policies but also can effectively and efficiently 'operationalise' them.

Increasingly we are seeing demands for a more open approach to government and consequently a need to actively build the trust and confidence of citizens and politicians in the Civil Service through accountability systems that underpin and encourage high performance.

We suggest that the next phase of the ongoing reform process should link the stakeholders' expectations of the Civil Service and the drivers for change discussed above, and focus on some key areas where that change can provide the greatest impact for improved performance.

It is informative in the first instance to consider briefly why these needs have not already been addressed through the DBG/SMI process of reform since its introduction in 1994. The requirement for statements of strategy, annual business plans and the Performance Management and Development System (PMDS), in theory at least, links the political policy requirements and department planning to the individual targets for delivery of the services required. It also provides for performance measurement in regard to these targets. Much has been achieved through this process.

However, in a number of areas progress has been slower than desired, and in some situations little progress has been made. This was highlighted by the PA Consulting Group (2002) review of the implementation of DBG/SMI, where it was noted that a 'debate on strategic HR had begun', and that the Management Information Framework was 'now in the process of being rolled out', though not yet fully availed of in many departments. The PA review also identified the issues of human resource management, financial management and information systems management as 'critical enablers of change', which needed to be addressed in a 're-energised and re-positioned' SMI/DBG.

To select the levers for this next phase of reform that will give greatest effect to the desired changes we should also look to experience abroad, where similar approaches to Civil Service reform have been adopted. The OECD report *Modernising Government: The Way Forward* (2005a) takes an overview of public sector governance by examining the trends in six levers of change in member countries over the past 20 years.

- Across the OECD member countries, governments are becoming more open, transparent, accessible and consultative. A continuing challenge for open government is to meet the higher expectations of citizens for more accessible and high-quality services and information.
- Enhancing public sector performance through performance management and budgeting is a widespread practice in most OECD countries.
- The trend in many countries in modernising accountability and control is seen in a move from *ex ante* to *ex post* control and the development of stronger internal control processes. This move creates a challenge to maintain control in systems where more delegation to third-party providers and agencies is the practice.
- Restructuring and reallocation of expenditure are identified as methods of responding to new policy priorities or to signal political intent to address a concern of citizens.
- The use of market-type mechanisms has become more common, although there are variations in this.

- People are a central resource of the Civil Service. The report examined the issue of organising and motivating public servants in terms of their conditions of employment, noting that early reformers who attempted such policies had underestimated the issue's complexity. However, it notes that remaining with the traditional arrangements 'is not a feasible option for most countries'.

Australia is recognised as one of the countries most advanced in public service reform. Much of that reform has centred on devolved public service structures, changes to human resources and leadership practices, and the appropriate accountability structures needed to accompany the increased devolution and flexibility. A report by the Australian Public Service Commission entitled *The Australian Experience of Public Sector Reform* examines many of these issues in some detail. It sees the challenges for the next phase of reform as including:

- the changing structure of government
- the changing environment of policy making, with greater involvement of stakeholders
- the need for enhanced performance and organisational capability
- devolution
- the need for better systems of accountability
- the need for a more coordinated whole-of-government approach and a unified Public Service defined by values.

The Australian government has divested itself of most state-run businesses and has moved from being an owner/manager of assets to becoming the standard-setter and the regulator. The remaining core government areas have been reformed to focus on performance. At the same time there is a commitment to avoid having a 'hollow government' where key skills are lost from the Civil Service through such policies. As a result there is significant emphasis on recruitment and on retention and development of staff skills, and a strong focus on the leadership capability framework.

Citizen and stakeholder involvement in the planning processes is also seen as an important challenge, as is the broader issue of globalisation. Arising from both the federal structure and extensive devolution over the past twenty years, there is a particular focus on the need for a whole-of-government approach with the development of new mechanisms and structures to facilitate this.

These themes have much in common with the position in New Zealand, and also parallel many of the issues of concern in Ireland.

Conclusions

In considering how best to create the conditions in the Irish Civil Service to allow departments and agencies to achieve the service delivery and performance levels required to meet the emerging challenges, we have sought to identify a number of key levers. The OECD suggests that among the factors important for future reform will be 'more open government, a focus on public sector performance, reforms to accountability and control, reallocation of resources in response to change, the introduction of market type mechanisms and reform of public employment systems'. It emphasises that there is an overwhelming case for adopting a whole-of-government perspective towards such reforms.

We largely concur with the OECD view, and we have therefore chosen to focus on the following subjects:

- organisational structures, including market mechanisms and agencification
- accountability systems, including the link to performance measurement
- leadership in the Civil Service, focusing on recruitment, reward and development.

Our choice of these particular issues was informed by our understanding of international trends and best practice, our analysis of stakeholder needs as articulated in this country, and detailed reflection on our own experience in Civil Service and public service organisations in Ireland. We do not suggest that these are the only issues that need to be addressed in the next phase of reform, but we are confident that any credible reform process will have to include them. While, of necessity, we address each of these areas seriatim in the following chapters, we would stress the need for an overall coherent strategic vision, and 'joined-up' implementation process, to drive future reform.

3

Reforming organisational structures to enhance performance and delivery within 'joined-up government'

This chapter explores structural arrangements within and between government bodies that are necessary to enhance public service performance and delivery. We focus in particular on measures to promote policy coherence and improved implementation within a whole-of-government context through exploring three key themes that we believe have a significant influence on how well public services are delivered: *department–agency relationships, market mechanisms,* and *reform at the centre.* But first, we consider a number of background issues to provide additional context to the three themes.

The recent OECD report *Modernising Government: The Way Forward* (2005) refers to organisational restructuring as 'the heavy machinery of reform', underlining that this type of reform is a major undertaking. It is difficult, time-consuming and resource-consuming. The impact can be felt both across and beyond the organisation. But to achieve fundamental and significant change, reform of organisational structures is sometimes the only effective option.

We selected the theme *department–agency relationships* because the creation of 'arm's length' bodies has been the most significant organisational change over the past quarter of a century in OECD countries. Ireland has pursued an agencification programme and today it has some 600 agencies, of which nearly 60 per cent have been established since 1990 (McGauran *et al.*, 2005). Ensuring alignment of service development and implementation is vital as the proportion of public services delivered by agencies increases. Deciding what organisational arrangements can best support corporate governance, drive cooperative behaviours and promote better connections is therefore fundamental. This section considers department and agency relationships in terms of governance, policy alignment and performance to support increased effectiveness and delivery of governmental objectives within a whole-of-government context.

The second theme is the use of *market mechanisms* to improve service performance and delivery. These encompass all arrangements where at least one significant characteristic of markets is present. The primary such mechanisms are outsourcing, public–private partnerships and vouchers. Using the market to deliver services in place of public bodies is a central tenet of New Public Management (NPM). This section reviews the use of market mechanisms in different countries. It discusses the assumptions underlying this approach and considers how the application of such measures could be improved in Ireland.

The significance of the challenge considered in the final theme, *reform at the centre*, which focuses on coordination and collaboration arrangements within and between departments in promoting a whole-of-government approach, is widely recognised and was an important factor in our decision to visit Australia and New Zealand. This section looks at what structures are required at the centre to ensure implementation and delivery, and considers to what extent the present central structures in Ireland are facilitating the development and achievement of departmental objectives. It also explores the ability of current cross-cutting mechanisms to provide the necessary coordination between and within departments and agencies.

The case for structural reform

Why change structures?

Governments change their organisational structures, according to the OECD (2005a), to respond to immediate public and political concerns, to give a higher priority to a particular policy, to improve the effectiveness of service delivery, or to reward a politician with a bigger department.

A variety of reasons why structural reforms have been pursued can be identified from the literature and from international experience, including the following.

- *Meeting demands for new public services* – particularly during periods of economic downturn – coupled with the adoption of NPM principles has been an important driver in the creation of agencies and the outsourcing of service provisions to private sector operators through market mechanisms.
- *Political responses to public concerns.* The rearrangement of functions between departments following a general election has been a trend in Ireland over the past 25 years or so. This can be very disruptive and impacts on service delivery. A variation is what the OECD calls 'confidence building', whereby a government announces a change to suggest something is being done, even if it takes a long time to implement.
- *The need to develop arrangements for policy coordination*, including creating cross-departmental groups and establishing dedicated coordination units within departments.
- *The pursuance of diversification, decentralisation and specialisation.*

The OECD (2005a) believes the pace at which societies are changing will require Governments increasingly to undertake restructuring as a means of delivering services. However, it calls for benefits and risks of organisational change to be carefully weighed before substantial change is proceeded with, including establishing those impacts that extend beyond the department involved.

Pursuing organisation change is difficult, disruptive, time consuming and can engender significant hostility from staff. To be successful it requires a very good reason for undertaking it, strong leadership, and political support. New structures must be thought out fully and a process put in place to gradually move to the desired end result.

The OECD (2005a) concluded that politically motivated change that gives the impression that something is happening now, can give very short-term gains but results in significant long-term costs. It believes the increasing trend of merging and separating department functions is likely to intensify because 'they are part of a Government's armoury of public persuasion' and to meet this challenge the Civil Service needs to be able to move to different functions both within the organisation and beyond to ensure that a whole-of-government perspective is maintained.

Some perspectives

Changing structural arrangements alone is unlikely to result in improved performance, and as such the measure is often associated with other change actions: for example, improving decision-making and leadership processes, refocusing accountability and control arrangements, redesigning programmes or changing levels of resources. It is appropriate to recall Kanter's (1983) view that the confluence of culture, participation and commitment as well as structure is necessary in effecting and consolidating change.

It is important to be clear in the first instance about what structural arrangements should address. Two perspectives serve to illustrate the breadth of the challenge. A recent Australian public service report, *Connecting Government* (2004), posed the fundamental question: 'if whole-of-government is the public service of the future how can structures help to achieve this?' An earlier Australian report (Coombs, 1976) concluded that a style of public administration was required that 'gives the citizen a greater sense of being in touch with decision-makers rather than an amorphous, unreachable department'. This challenge is equally relevant today.

It is also important to consider organisational structural changes from both internal and external perspectives – the former relates to changes within an organisation; examples of the latter are agencification, contracting-out of services and privatisation. Significant changes invariably affect both the internal and external arrangements. Thus, establishing a new agency calls for new governance arrangements to be established within the primary department.

There is no such thing as a 'one-size-fits-all' solution to challenges common to different administrations. The environment will invariably differ significantly in terms of administrative forms, culture and experience. With the possible exceptions of the health and education services (although some would question this), the tendency in Ireland has been to maintain a relatively centralised form of government, with departments delivering a significant portion of public services directly. This can be contrasted with Sweden and Finland, where the tradition of a strong local decentralised government framework extends back over many centuries. Central government in these two countries is small in comparison to other OECD countries and is focused on policy formulation and a number of national-level issues such as foreign relations and defence.

There are also significant differences in how countries go about implementing similar measures or programmes: the OECD (2005a) highlights the successful agencification programmes in the UK, the Netherlands and New Zealand, where the approaches adopted in setting up and operating such bodies were very different in each country. Success depends on the particular political and administrative cultures prevailing.

Although Ireland has experienced agencification and significant structural changes in a limited number of bodies, such as the Revenue Commissioners and the Department of Social and Family Affairs, the main focus of the SMI is on strengthening management capability at all levels, modernising human resource management (HRM) and financial management systems, expanding IT use, and enhancing transparency, accountability and regulation. Before SMI one of the most significant efforts to change internal departmental structures was the recommendation of the Devlin Report (1966–1969) relating to the creation of an *aireacht* separate from executive functions. This did not, of course, change the traditional hierarchical structure of a department.

Reflections on the traditional bureaucracy

Despite the significant public sector reforms since the 1980s, the traditional hierarchical structure within public sector organisations has remained strong. A reluctance to tamper with the traditional arrangements appears to be widely shared, and prevailing political, administrative and social cultures continue to represent major challenges to radical internal organisational change.

The machine bureaucracy as described by Mintzberg (2003) has been the fundamental operating structure for Civil Service organisations. This design fulfilled the requirement for efficiency, reliability, consistency and precision for government operations in a stable environment. Modern demands for flexibility, responsiveness, innovation and service tailored to the individual have stimulated discussions on the suitability of the machine organisation. Some in the private sector maintain that the traditional hierarchy has tended to inhibit innovations and that companies gain competitive advantage by being the first to fashion the new organisational form that best capitalises on new emerging technologies for the customers' needs (Herbert *et al.*, 2000). Kanter (1990) proposed that winning in modern business requires more speed, flexibility and creativity than is found in the traditional bureaucracy, and management needs the freedom to pursue opportunities without the burden of cumbersome structures and unnecessary procedures.

However, the arguments for keeping the machine bureaucracy are compelling. Jacques (1990) considers that managerial hierarchy is the most efficient and the hardiest structure ever devised for large organisations. He suggests that a hierarchy meets the fundamental needs of adding value to work as it moves through the organisation, nailing down accountability, placing people with the necessary competencies at each organisational layer, and building an acceptance of the managerial structure that achieves these ends. Leavitt (2003) agrees, and suggests that it is 'sensible to accept the reality that hierarchies are here to stay and work hard to reduce their highly noxious by-products, while making them more habitable for humans and more productive as well'.

It is also important to recognise the OECD's caution (2005) that in developing new approaches to organisation agility a balance must be struck between the value and contribution of the traditional public service hierarchical structures and the importance of going beyond mere consensus-building that is often attendant on cross-departmental and agency interactions.

Coordination and subordination

Balancing coordination and subordination is an essential feature of modern government structures in view of the 'fragmented' nature of service delivery across many organisational forms. The OECD (2005a) expressed the current organisational challenge as 'how to organise the public sector so that it can adapt to the changing needs of society, without losing coherence of strategy or continuity of governance values'. Countries that have recognised these difficulties have looked for ways of strengthening the centre while still giving managers the freedom to manage.

One of the dominant concepts of NPM is the separation of the organisational centre from service delivery to improve effectiveness. Rose and Lawton (1999) define decentralisation in terms of 'power transferred from a central body to sub-units or operational agencies. The centre gives up some of its power and decisions are taken lower down the hierarchical organisation.' Proponents of decentralisation argue that it increases flexibility and responsiveness as well as being more democratic. This restructuring of the public services is described by Winstanley *et al.* (1995) as involving a change to localised management of service provision, arm's-length regulation, complex networks, contracting-out of services, development of quasi-markets, and splitting of the purchaser and provider roles. This leaves the centre's role, as described by Bahrami (1992), as being to 'orchestrate the broad strategic vision, develop the shared organizational and administrative infrastructure, and create the cultural glue which can create synergies, and ensure unity of mission and purpose'. Leslie and Tilley (2004) recommend a regular review of the activities of the centre to assess whether greater value would be created by moving them elsewhere in the organisation, leaving only 'shaping' and 'safeguarding' activities at the centre.

A downside to this 'decentralisation' has been fragmentation of the public sector with a proliferation of independently minded agencies, resulting in duplication of effort, overlapping roles, pursuit of competing interests and territoriality. The National Economic and Social Council (NESC) (2006) identified additional difficulties arising from the tendency to formulate objectives around what can be measured and ignoring what is difficult to measure, the need to recognise the importance of quality as well as cost effectiveness, and the continuation of interference from the centre. In instances where there was good separation of policy from delivery, NESC also observed a problem with policy formulation losing the insight gained from the interaction with the service user.

The *Review of the Centre* carried out in New Zealand in 2001 also identified problems associated with multiple agencies, which included the following.

- Difficulties in coordinating service delivery increase costs and blur accountability.
- There is a risk of reduced capacity through spreading leadership talent and skills over a greater number of agencies.
- Ministers need to build relationships with a greater number of organizations.
- Alignment of fragmented organisations is more difficult.

The UK think-tank Reform (Darwall, 2005) has expressed the view that a successor to the seminal *Next Steps* (1988) report, the *Modernising Government* white paper of 1999, failed to identify the importance of structure, linked to incentives and accountability, as the means to secure agency performance. *Modernising Government* emphasises institutionalised cross-agency collaboration as the key to achieving whole-of-government delivery, which Reform scathingly dismisses as 'long on ends and desperately short on means'.

At the core of Reform's argument, and central to NPM, is a combination of *letting* and *making* managers manage through a clear separation of roles and accountability for performance. Reform regrets the current UK trend of re-strengthening the central role of departments in ensuring implementation, or 'turning departments into corporate head offices of their delivery arms' (Darwall, 2005, p. 27).

Summary

Reforming organisational structures to enhance performance and delivery within joined-up government is a major undertaking but is often necessary to achieve fundamental change, which the OECD believes governments will increasingly undertake. However, since changing structural arrangements alone is unlikely to result in improved performance, it is often associated with other change actions such as improving decision-making and leadership processes and refocusing accountability and control arrangements.

Since 1980 significant agencification and outsourcing of service provision has taken place internationally; Ireland too has pursued substantial agencification since 1990. Effective coordination arrangements that do not undermine local management within devolved structures are necessary. Although Ireland differs in some respects from other OECD countries, the challenge of ensuring alignment between policy development and delivery through arm's-length arrangements is shared. How departments establish, govern and oversee the performance of agencies, and how they manage and oversee outsourcing through market mechanisms, is central to the effectiveness of public service delivery. Deciding what arrangements can best support corporate governance and cooperative behaviours is fundamental.

While Mintzberg's traditional machine bureaucracy remains the fundamental operating structure for the public service, collaboration and coordination arrangements are needed at all levels of government for a whole-of-service response. Effective arrangements within and between departments are no less important than department–agency governance arrangements to avoid poorly planned, fragmented and badly delivered services. Using the strength of the machine bureaucracy, an appropriate balance between coordination and subordination imperatives can motivate and channel the efforts of the different actors for high performance within agreed service objective frameworks.

Department–agency relationships

Agencification: the main structural reform to date

The creation of agencies has been the most significant organisational change over the past quarter of a century in OECD countries. The OECD (2005a) makes the point that although the circumstances differ from country to country, the reasons for establishing agencies are for the most part shared. These include:

- the view that traditional centralised government bureaucracies are a bad thing
- the desire to free operational managers from politically oriented government departments – letting managers manage in line with NPM principles
- adopting private sector practices and simpler structures that separate perceived conflicting responsibilities, such as policy-making, delivery and regulation.

While the Scandinavian countries have a long tradition of agencification and the UK, the Netherlands and New Zealand have successfully created agencies over the past 20 years, the OECD stresses that there are huge differences in the way the agencies work in each of these countries. According to the OECD, the UK established many agencies during the Thatcher government years in order to curtail local authority powers: this had huge consequences for the delivery of local services, accountability arrangements, transparency and citizen participation, as well as demotivating local authority public representatives and staff.

Experiences in New Zealand and Australia

New Zealand followed the NPM path of extensive agencification during the early years of its reform process. The OECD (2005a) reports that agencies account for over 80 per cent of state employees and some 60 per cent of public expenditure. However, following dispersal and devolution of public services in the early years of reform, the focus now is on integrating and linking the elements. Humphreys *et al.* (1999) note that a review of New Zealand reforms carried out by Holmes and Wileman in 1995 concluded that the over-separation of policy and service delivery had a number of adverse affects. During our visit to New Zealand we were informed that no new agencies are currently being set up, and it is not planned for the time being to privatise more public services delivery; this is part of an ongoing wider retrenchment process to strengthen central government capability and enhance joined-up service planning and provision.

Australia didn't follow New Zealand and other OECD countries in pursuing widespread agency establishment. While it pursued reforms common to most OECD countries relating to strategic planning and management and better financial, HR and IT systems, Australia placed particular emphasis on the application of market principles to the delivery of public services. Following the Hilmer report (1993), competition and contestability based on market principles became a central tenet of public service delivery. Outsourcing of public services was adopted on a significant scale. Following a recognition that the process of coordinating across multiple portfolios would never be easy, the adoption in 1987 of a policy of reducing the number of government portfolios resulted in a small number of larger departments and 'super' agencies. *Connecting Government* (2004) highlights the significance of this step – 'larger portfolios make coordination easier'. This policy pertains today.

It should have been expected, then, that in the wake of significant programmes of devolution and decentralisation, attention would inevitably turn to coordinating and linking services. Over the past few years initiatives have been pursued in both countries to achieve this. The Uhrig report (2003) in Australia and the strengthening of the 'statement of intent' strategic planning framework in New Zealand (State Services Commission, 2005) are examples of such initiatives, and are discussed in more detail below. Assigning responsibility to secretaries general and chief executives for oversight of total public service delivery in geographically defined areas is another example of how the whole-of-government challenge in both countries is being tackled creatively.

Agencification in Ireland

A review of non-commercial agencies in Ireland by McGauran *et al.* (2005) identified the main reasons for the establishment of agencies here, as follows.

- *Economic and efficiency reasons* – avoiding bureaucratic 'red tape' and adopting private sector principles.
- *Changing societal expectations* – the public expect to receive services analogous to those provided by the private sector.
- *Political reasons* – reducing political input into decision-making or to enable politicians to demonstrate that something is happening.
- *Specialisation* – bringing together expertise not normally available in the Civil Service, e.g. environment protection.
- *Isomorphic factors* – 'everyone else is doing it'.

McGauran *et al.* (2005) report that two-thirds of Ireland's 600 non-commercial national agencies have been set up through legislation. These agencies carry out a range of functions that fall into three main categories – implementation, advisory and regulatory. McGauran *et al.* also make the point that, unlike the international scenario, agencies in Ireland provide policy advice. Very few of them are engaged in the delivery of core public services, while a great many were established specifically to provide specialist services. Agencies are not evenly spread across sectors: many exist in areas such as local government and environment, health and community affairs, while very few exist in agriculture. McGauran *et al.* report very significant variations in the criteria used for establishing agencies, in governance and reporting arrangements, in board membership and in management structures and related matters. Similarly, approaches adopted by departments to establishing agency budgets, service level agreements and general working arrangements vary considerably.

This can be contrasted with the process of establishing agencies in the wake of the 1988 UK *Next Steps* initiative, in which a comprehensive eight-stage establishment process was followed. The purpose of the process was first to examine the need for the agency and whether there were alternative ways of performing the work or achieving the mission of the proposed body. Other stages sought to clarify agency objectives, performance targets, and review and reporting arrangements. An important point was that these steps had to be completed before a board was appointed. While the agencies established under this process may *de jure* be 'executive units' closely linked to – if not within – departments, the CEO is appointed by open competition and is accountable directly to the minister.

As noted above, joining up government through creating stronger links between the centre and periphery remains a key target in New Zealand and Australia. However, an important distinction between those countries (and many other OECD countries) and Ireland is that, with the exception of the health services, Ireland didn't devolve core public services such as social services to the same extent. A tradition of strong centralised government coupled with a large number of relatively small local authorities may have been relevant here. A high proportion of new Irish agencies established since 1990 have been small, stand-alone, service-specific bodies. Thus, New Zealand and Australia are working from a very dispersed service delivery scenario to recreate lost links, while Ireland retains the capacity to link up and coordinate different service strands more easily, whether or not this is implemented.

Foundation stones for good department–agency relationships

Countries approach the establishment of agencies in different ways – some by administrative processes and others by legislation. The OECD (2005a) reports that some countries act in a piecemeal manner and set up agencies when the situation is deemed 'ripe' to do so, while others go through a more structured process. Although the issue of how establishment happens is important in terms of their roles, degree of independence and subsequent relationship with the minister, Schick (2001) stresses the criticality of addressing governance and accountability questions before agencies are established, as retrofitting such practices can be difficult.

Whatever the motivation for the establishment of agencies, Schick has identified a number of interrelated challenges in terms of placing the department–agency relationship on an appropriate footing.

- *The need to strike a balance between coordination and subordination,* i.e. ensuring agency independence with accountability.
- *How governance should be pursued for performance.* Schick stresses the importance of paying less attention to motive and more to overall impact in assessing agency performance, since agencies will always pursue their own agendas.
- *Difficulties in linking policies to execution.* Functional integration can be secured where services are delivered directly by the centre; the danger of service providers failing to comply with government policies is higher in a fragmented scenario.

Having regard to this perspective and drawing on experience from the visit to Australia and New Zealand, we considered the requirements for a positive department–agency relationship in the following terms:

- the governance challenge
- policy alignment/coordination and subordination
- securing agency performance.

Before addressing these in turn, it is valuable to recall two recent Australian reports that provide an insight into the development and operation of agencies. *Connecting Government* (2004), which provides guidance on agencies operating within a whole-of-government framework, states that 'At the heart of best practice for agency arrangements is the careful definition of the task, agreement on the respective roles and resourcing, attention to legal powers of constraints, adequate training and an effective means for monitoring and managing the arrangement.'

The Uhrig report (2003) developed a template of governance principles and best practice for Australian statutory agencies and office-holders following consideration of public and private sector practices. Uhrig focused on six principles to guide the establishment of agencies (unlike the UK *Next Steps* report (1988), which focused on process). The principles are as follows.

- Owners, or their representatives, need to establish a clear understanding of success for the activity, including their expectations of performance.
- Governance should be present and the arrangements should be appropriate for the entity given the nature of ownership and functions.
- To be successful, power must be in existence, delegated, limited and exercised.
- There should be clarity of roles within the governance arrangements of organisations.
- With responsibility there needs to be accountability.
- For a board to be effective, it must have the full power to act, including the ability to appoint, supervise and remove senior management as well as approve strategy.

A valuable contribution to agency structures and governance in the Irish context is a report prepared by Prospectus for the Department of Health and Children in 2003 relating to an audit of structures and functions in the health system. The central thrust of this report was the need to consolidate fragmented structures and functions within a whole-of-health context, including a significant reduction in the number of agencies.

Prospectus argued (p. 45) that not only did the proliferation of agencies make oversight difficult for the parent department, but

> a more pertinent concern lies in the fact that the work of some agencies has extended beyond their original remit, which has led to duplication and a lack of pooling of expertise and know-how. Most critically, it has also led to an almost unmanageable mix of agenda-setting institutions with a strong focus but often lacking a broad policy context.

While recognising that the health services present a particular problem in Ireland, the findings of McGauran *et al.* (2005) confirm that similar problems exist in other departments where multiple agencies exist.

Prospectus also highlights the importance of strengthening the functioning of the consolidated structure through the development of supporting processes such as service planning, improving service delivery evaluation, and measures to promote integration. It calls for strengthening of governance and accountability arrangements across the board. Prospectus identifies a number of elements that have general application to underpin the effective operation of the consolidated structure, including:

- clear accountability lines throughout the system
- a national focus for integrating service delivery
- continuous quality improvement and increased external appraisal
- robust information-gathering and analysis capability.

Follow-up measures to Prospectus include proposals to reduce and amalgamate existing agencies. A similar process (on a wider scale) was noted in Victoria, Australia, which included reducing the number of government departments to ten and amalgamation of a large number of agencies.

The barriers to consolidating agencies within appropriate frameworks are considerable, such as weak political support and resistance from 'independence-oriented' agencies themselves. Yet to enhance delivery through reduced fragmentation, improved coordination and simpler operational arrangements, the provision of coherent consolidated service frameworks similar to that proposed for the health services, in which the minimum number of independent public bodies are supported, is important. The implementation of such frameworks should be accompanied by a programme to reduce the number of agencies as well as the introduction of periodic reviews of the continued relevance and performance of existing agencies.

The case for utilising an executive office structure within a department as an alternative to the agency route to deliver front-line services should be an important consideration. Examples of this form include the Centre for Management and Organisational Development (CMOD) in the Department of Finance, the Social Welfare Office in the Department of Social and Family Affairs, and Irish Aid in the Department of Foreign Affairs. An executive office would present fewer problems in aligning policy; it would enable policy-makers to maintain close links to the front line while separate budget lines from the parent department would facilitate accountability. The department would also enjoy greater HR mass and thus greater flexibility in delivering on its remit. The minister, however, would retain responsibility for the office and Civil Service employment conditions would apply. Ostensibly, an executive office may offer less operational flexibility than an independent agency, although in the case of a single-task agency this is certainly questionable. The opportunity to leverage the benefits of a private sector service delivery approach might be more difficult to realise.

The governance challenge

The Prospectus report (2003) serves to underline the OECD's (2005) conclusions that the existence of multiple agencies leads to difficulties in coordinating public services, resulting in overlapping and duplication of work as well as a lack of coherence in delivery. A reduction in democratic control and accountability, including a reduced capacity to measure performance, is also seen as a significant challenge. The presence of other stakeholders on agency boards can exacerbate these difficulties. Prospectus (2003) also alludes to difficulties arising through agencies pursuing their own agendas.

The OECD (2005a) suggests a number of conditions to ensure a successful and sustainable distributed agency governance system. This includes having a sound legal and institutional framework that provides a clear operational framework and acts to limit the number of bodies created. The OECD also calls for a well-thought-out organisational structure as well as a phasing-in process in the establishment of the agency that facilitates the introduction of good governance, steering and reporting arrangements.

The key governance challenges identified by the New Zealand State Services Commission (2003) include:

- unclear expectations of the roles and responsibilities of all actors
- accountability arrangements that are inconsistent across the agencies
- apparent lack of a public sector ethos
- uneven monitoring of agencies by the centre/ ministers.

McGauran *et al.* (2005) present evidence for similar governance challenges in Ireland, although it is arguable that the public sector ethos remains generally strong here. They highlight an excessive focus on HR and finance inputs to the detriment of accountability for outputs. They also cite board composition and the absence of a coherent approach to the establishment of agencies as significant issues to be addressed here. The Prospectus report (2003) points to the need for boundaries between agencies (particularly in relation to shared services), the importance of grounding non-financial performance accountability in legislation, and (again) the composition and role of boards.

While the critical role of an agency board is generally recognised, significant differences are evident in board composition and how board roles and accountability are viewed. There is wide agreement in principle on the need for members to possess appropriate experience and for the adoption of a board size that supports effective working arrangements. Uhrig (2003) stresses the importance of giving boards full powers to act, but also concludes that representational appointments 'have the potential to place the success of the entity at risk'.

There is no common approach to representational arrangements on Irish agency boards, and a variety of practices have grown up. In many instances, e.g. the fisheries boards, statutory provisions underpin representation. In view of the strength of the Partnership ethos in Ireland today, representational arrangements on boards might be expected. However, the appropriateness of such arrangements needs to be considered in the context of both the contribution and threats to agencies, taking on board Uhrig's (2003) position as well as experience of such arrangements in Ireland to date. Where representational interests on boards are maintained, clarity and transparency around agency outcome and performance expectations are essential to keep all board members focused on a shared agenda. A number of these issues are addressed below.

To undertake an effective governance role, departments must have appropriate capabilities to do the job. Both McGauran *et al.* (2005) and Uhrig (2003) stress the importance of suitable departmental structures and strengthened capacity to undertake the role effectively. Uhrig calls for a central function or group to advise on the application of appropriate governance and legislative structures when agencies are established and reviewed. McGauran *et al.* call for the establishment of appropriately skilled 'governance of agencies' units in departments focused on goal-setting, monitoring and evaluation. In 2006 the Taoiseach announced the government's intention to have an external review of structures, capacities, procedures and leadership of departments and agencies. This presents an ideal opportunity to address departments' capacities to undertake an effective governance role.

McGauran *et al.* (2005) also suggest that consideration be given to departmental participation at a senior level on boards. Some departments adopted an approach similar to that of the then Department of the Marine and Natural Resources, of not appointing officials to boards because of possible conflicts of interest with the governance role and in relation to financial and HR management issues. A different approach is adopted in the Department of Agriculture, Food and Forestry. There, a senior official is a member of the Teagasc Board to facilitate policy alignment between centre and agency. Australia and New Zealand promote departmental participation on agency boards in the context of whole-of-government coordination, where the governance emphasis is more on performance delivery than on detailed control of financial and HR issues. This approach might facilitate a more productive departmental participation on boards here, but it doesn't address key questions relating to conflict over duties of board members and the governance role.

Policy alignment/coordination and subordination

Policy alignment is about ensuring that government policies are fully implemented between the centre and periphery irrespective of the organisational structures or delivery arrangements in place. Policies need to be developed, implemented, monitored and reported on in a whole-of-government context at all levels. Schick (2001) highlights the necessity of restraining and empowering both policy-makers and service deliverers to ensure the right balance between coordination and subordination on the one hand and independence and flexibility on the other. In drawing organisational boundaries between the centre and agency, the needs of promoting policy coherence must be paramount.

The governance approach or style adopted by departments is important. Peters (2006) draws a distinction between two ostensibly competing views of future governance arrangements: returning to a more rigid form or continuing with a softer form that has been promoted in recent years. The former is characterised by a recentralising of government, often in the context of ensuring delivery of central objectives. Here the concept of steering is important. The current trend in the UK could be said to exhibit characteristics of this approach. A softer form of governance relies more on cooperation and collaboration, on guidelines rather than on rules, in which partnership is valued. This form may encourage agency engagement and local participation but can create difficulties relating to responsibility and delivery of central objectives. A balance between the two approaches is ultimately necessary.

Uhrig (2003), echoing Schick's views on the overriding need to address governance and accountability questions formally in department–agency relations, calls for direct linkages to be created between central and agency policies. Uhrig recommends that ministers should issue public 'statements of expectations', with statutory bodies responding with 'statements of intent' (SOIs). These set out specific outcomes to be achieved and, in our view, go beyond the statement of strategies currently prepared by departments in Ireland. Uhrig also recommends that requiring statutory authorities and office-holders to provide relevant information should reinforce the role of departments.

Successful devolution of power to managers at the front line needs a clear accountability framework and should have regard to the principles of public accountability. The SOI that all crown entities in New Zealand must prepare describes the nature and scope of the entity's function, what it is trying to achieve (including why and how it will do it), along with the financial and non-financial measures and standards that will be used to assess progress. An important element is that *before* the agency SOI is adopted it is audited by the parent department for policy alignment. This brings an independent perspective on the appropriateness and match of the proposed agency programme to government policies rather than relying on the more usual *ex post* audits and reviews. This differs in a number of ways from the Irish process of formulating strategy statements, including in the degree of scrutiny of the strategy for alignment with government policy, in the clarity of performance indicators and their relationship to outcomes, and in the degree of accountability for achievement. The New Zealand State Services Commission also reviews and reports on the performance of public service chief executives and their departments.

Aside from departmental participation in agency boards (see above), we noted in both Australia and New Zealand the importance placed on periodic meetings of all sector-wide agency CEOs and regular meetings with departmental management boards to promote policy alignment and services delivery. This approach helps to encourage strategic sectoral leadership. Moreover, under best practice guidance from the New Zealand Controller and Auditor General, single lead agencies, common outcome statements and joint consultation processes are among the measures advocated to promote whole-of-government approaches through shared actions by agencies.

In his consideration of the boundaries between the roles of service provision and policy analysis, Schick (2001) makes the important point that 'much of what parades as policy analysis these days deals with efficiency in the provision of services. Policy analysts compare the costs and benefits of services of alternative delivery systems; they do not have much role in setting the boundaries.' Awareness of this distinction is important both in framing and reviewing policies and in converting policies adopted into service delivery programmes.

Securing agency performance

We noted in Australia and New Zealand the importance attached to how agencies are monitored and evaluated as part of a general drive to ensure effective and efficient delivery of public services. Where services are delivered through the market, the normal market mechanisms such as tendering can provide significant assistance in ensuring value for money. Assessing agency performance is more difficult, especially in non-commercial sectors. Having the right assessment framework, the right information and the political will to follow through in addressing poor performance is critical. We also noted the very high priority accorded at all levels in both countries to progressing the definition and use of *outcome* targets and related performance indicators.

Linking service and budgetary planning to performance outcomes (expressed through indicators) and establishing strong links between service delivery and evaluation are among the most significant challenges in improving agency performance assessment. The importance of robust perform-ance information is emphasised in an Australian National Audit Office (ANAO) publication, *Better Practice in Annual Performance Reporting*, issued in 2004. ANAO makes the point that to improve performance:

1 strategies must be pursued to establish a robust perform-ance culture based on public services values
2 strong links between reporting, planning and manage-ment need to be maintained
3 links between external and internal reporting need to be developed.

ANAO asserts that without transparent high-quality information within an appropriate internal and external reporting frame-work, oversight of agency performance will be significantly impaired. The New Zealand State Services Commission (2003) also highlights in particular the importance of *disclo-sure* and *transparency* within agency arrangements, both to underpin governance and to make management and the board answerable. Disclosure provisions, including data quality and coherence standards, are explicitly incorporated in service-level agreements (SLAs), memoranda of under-standing (MOUs), and periodic reporting requirements.

McGauran *et al.* (2005, pp. 119–120) highlight the pre-dominance in Irish agencies of financial reporting over non-financial activity reporting, and they conclude that reporting on non-financial targets is generally very weak. The issue of the availability of non-financial information in the Irish public services is dealt with in greater detail in Chapter 4.

The Council on Cost and Quality of Government in New South Wales is a body that examines and reports on agency performance and cross-sectoral issues, and promotes better management practices. The NSW government has a policy of regularly reviewing, through the Council, the appropriateness, efficiency, effectiveness and prudence of its agencies and programmes. The council monitors the implementation of its recommendations and periodically reports on progress to cabinet.

The context for performance assessment is very important, particularly in assessing whole-of-government achievement. The recent government decision to strengthen the Expenditure Review Initiative (ERI) underlines the importance of, *inter alia*, taking a sectoral impact into account in assessing value for money and policy implementation. Both Australia and New Zealand have adopted polices of ensuring that agency SOIs include whole-of-government objectives and these are assessed as part of the performance review process. Transparency in reporting agency performance is also very important to promoting a culture of performance. We noted that under the new ERI arrangements, reports must be published except in the most exceptional circumstances.

Market mechanisms

The strategies employed by different countries in bringing about public sector reform have been characterised by Schick (1999) in terms of:

1 *the market approach*, which seeks to draw a sharp distinction between the state as policy-maker and the state as service provider
2 *a managerial model*, which allows for a broader role for government in providing public services but wants these activities to be less hobbled by bureaucratic rules and more sensitive to the wants of recipients
3 *a programme strategy*, where the state produces desired social outcomes within severe resource constraints
4 *an incremental model*, where the state continues to function along familiar lines but is less burdened by old rules and requirements.

Some countries are very clear in adopting a particular approach, such as New Zealand, where market-like arrangements predominate. Ireland's approach has been characterised as conforming primarily to the managerial model, but in reality it is a hybrid, with many elements of the market approach being increasingly employed.

Appeal of market mechanisms

Market mechanisms have penetrated core public services in most OECD countries. This arose out of the conservative belief that government services are inherently inefficient, that the private sector is more flexible and adaptive, and that significant efficiency gains can be achieved though the use of such mechanisms. By shifting services away from central government, the size of the public sector is perceived to be reduced and responsibility for the actual quality of service delivery is shifted at least in part from the centre – an important political consideration. At this point there is substantial evidence to support the general tenet behind marketisation in terms of reduced costs or better services, but the position is not as simple as originally proposed. There are significant challenges for governments in applying market-type mechanisms and moving from the role of provider to purchaser of services. Particular concerns have been raised in regard to governance issues in terms of accountability, transparency, regularity, and the access to redress mechanisms for citizens (OECD, 2005a).

Types of market mechanisms

Market-type mechanisms encompass all arrangements where at least one significant characteristic of markets is present. They include outsourcing, public–private partnerships and vouchers. Privatisation in the sense of 'selling off' state enterprises is the ultimate route to the market for established enterprises such as utilities or airlines. However, once this has taken place the traditional role of the state in terms of regulation or oversight is effectively removed.

Competition is the key market characteristic. From empirical evidence it now appears that few services cannot be provided through market mechanisms, but clearly some areas are more amenable to this approach than others. In 1991, de Coninck-Smith proposed a privatisation matrix for identifying government services that were most amenable to competition and NPM-type restructuring. Many new examples of core state service provision through market mechanisms have been seen in recent years.

Public–private partnerships (PPPs)

PPPs are arrangements whereby the private sector designs, builds, finances, maintains and operates large infrastructure assets traditionally provided by the public sector. They are most appealing for large-scale projects that involve extensive maintenance and operating requirements over the project's 'whole-of-life'. They typically include transportation infrastructure and the provision of public buildings such as schools and hospitals. In some instances they have involved the purchase of existing infrastructure, but they generally apply to the provision and maintenance of new facilities for a specified 'lifetime'.

The potential advantages of PPPs are cost efficiency through competition, transference of risk away from government, and availability of private sector expertise. Competitive tendering ensures keen pricing. The risk of construction overruns, additional costs or technical deficiency risks can be transferred in large part to the private partner – though this will in turn be reflected in the cost. Availability risk in terms of standards and quality of service to the customer can also be reduced for government. In general, risk management can be better allocated to the party with the greatest control over that risk. Demand risk must also be carefully managed, as this can provide benefits as well as shortfalls, as in the case of Dublin's West Link Bridge. Opponents of PPPs will argue, however, that there is little empirical evidence to date of any significant risk transference.

Where PPPs involve 'whole-of-life' perspectives there are

inherent incentives for the private partner to provide quality in both the design and building phases of development. Also in this regard it is crucial that the private partner provide the project financing in order to have the proper incentives and assume the appropriate risks.

Some initial PPPs were piloted in Ireland in 1999, followed a year or so later by a major review of the implementation procedures that then applied. Not all PPPs have demonstrated advantages over conventional government procurement procedures. The Comptroller & Auditor General's report in 2004 on the apparently successful Grouped Schools Pilot Partnership Project concluded that the original public procurement cost comparison, which had calculated a lifetime cost saving of 6 per cent, had in fact erred and that the true comparison was a 13 to 19 per cent excess over comparable public procurement costs. Subsequent to this a national policy framework for PPPs and a number of support structures were developed to guide the selection and implementation of such projects (Irish Government PPP website). The support structures included a Central PPP Unit responsible for overall coordination and a National Development Finance Agency to finance major public projects and to evaluate financing options for PPP projects.

One crucial issue in relation to PPPs is the difficulty in comparing the costs of PPP procurement and conventional procurement of the same project, so as to decide whether or not PPP represents value for money. A second issue is that the complexity of PPP deals means that the procurement costs can be substantially higher than the costs of conventional procurement.

New measures to ensure value for money with conventional procurement contracts were announced by the Minister for Finance in October 2005. These included both structural and process change. If they are equally effective in reducing costs and risks associated with these types of contracts, then the claimed comparative advantages of PPPs may be even further reduced.

In conclusion, we believe that the use of PPPs needs to be kept under review. PPPs initially were not particularly successful and became advantageous only after the process was subjected to detailed scrutiny and development. Conventional procurement procedures should be redeveloped along the same lines as those applying to PPPs, with a view to providing more effective and efficient outcomes. This in turn would influence the selection of preferred procurement procedure (PPP versus conventional).

Outsourcing

Outsourcing is increasingly being adopted as a means of delivering public services in OECD countries. It is typically found in the provision of 'blue collar' services such as cleaning, facilities management, waste management, food services and guard services. Increasingly, high-value professional services such as IT, legal, HR and banking/financial services are being outsourced. These are often complex and involve rapid change in their operating environment. The extreme examples of outsourcing in terms of core government activities are found in the provision of prison services in the USA, the UK, Canada and Australia and in the services of the Audit Office in New Zealand. Outsourced services can be provided to government departments/agencies or directly to citizens. Advantages claimed include cost efficiency and more flexible access to expertise that is not readily available within existing government departments. In some instances outsourcing has been adopted as a remedy for poor performance by existing public sector providers.

Outsourcing may be based on a standard competitive tendering process or on a set of qualifying suppliers, allowing users a choice of supplier through a voucher scheme. In some OECD countries it is now mandatory to market-test options for the provision of services and to evaluate alternatives with private sector providers, before determining the provision of new services.

The capacity of government to outsource effectively needs to be developed and sustained over time. The commercial competence necessary for managing the outsourcing process must be developed. Delivering services at arm's length presents particular governance difficulties in terms of supervision and quality control. Retaining the technical expertise of the function being outsourced is often essential both in regard to these governance issues and also for essential contingency purposes. We learned that in one New Zealand regional council, all relevant engineering expertise within the authority was lost to the private sector as a result of outsourcing policy. This left the authority with no capacity for performance assessment or governance. Maintaining this capacity has implications for human resource management and internal structures, and can represent additional overheads that are not always taken into account in the outsourcing value for money equation.

Transparency can be reduced with outsourcing, as the public's right to access information may be diminished. In addition, the redress developed for the public sector in terms of an ombudsman, FOI and whistleblower mechanisms will not apply to private sector providers. For outsourcing to be successful, competitive supplier markets are essential, and so governments must develop and sustain such markets for these services.

Vouchers

Vouchers separate the provision of services from their financing (Blondal, 2005). They facilitate choice and competition for the customer. The government pays the provider directly. Vouchers are specific to given services, they may allow for recovery for all or some of the costs of the service/goods, eligibility can be determined separately, and the actual service can be provided jointly by public and private sector providers. The form of voucher can vary from physical coupons to electronic smart cards. The use of vouchers is largely associated with the provision of social and medical services, education or housing supplements for low-income families.

Conceptually there are three main forms of voucher application. An explicit voucher is a physical coupon or smart card that facilitates the transaction between the recipient and the supplier, and subsequently that between the supplier and the government body. An implicit voucher is where the qualifying recipient registers with one of a number of designated suppliers and the government pays directly to that provider of the service (e.g., medical card). The third form is where the government reimburses the user for expenditures on qualifying services from approved suppliers.

Housing assistance vouchers can help avoid the creation of ghetto-type state-provided low-cost housing estates, allowing participants to position themselves within the commercial housing sector. Implicit vouchers can ensure a uniform level of tuition between state and private schools, where fees are allowed only in respect of non-tuition expenditures. Tax credits for specific childcare expenditures are also a form of voucher.

The payment structure of vouchers can influence the behaviour of suppliers. They pose unique challenges in terms of design and contextual factors. They are demand-driven and based on eligibility factors and so can exert an upward pressure on public expenditure. As a market mechanism for the provision of public services they have advantages over conventional centrally provided services, but they must be well designed and managed to avoid inherent weaknesses.

Delivering market approaches

Efficiency gains associated with market-type mechanisms can be substantial in terms of reduced costs, better-quality services or improved resource allocation at national economy level. However, there is often significant resistance from staff within existing public service providers, such that these mechanisms are often easier to introduce for new services or projects.

There is also a need to develop arrangements and capabilities for governance of these mechanisms. This includes transparency, accountability, regulatory processes and the availability of avenues of redress. There is the risk, however, of governments becoming beholden to suppliers once their own capacity to provide the service is lost. In many situations the optimal position seems to be for a government to retain the expertise and capacity to provide some portion of the services directly.

Reform at the centre: structures for implementation and monitoring

The Irish position

Historically, there has been an absence of centralised departmental coordination in Ireland, but this changed in 1994 following the establishment of the Coordinating Group of Secretaries to deliver the SMI modernisation agenda. Two years later the Coordinating Group produced its comprehensive document *Delivering Better Government* (DBG). This document highlighted the importance of a strategic framework to achieve consistency and coherence in realising the objectives of government. It recommended the development of strategic results areas to identify the key priority issues and detail the required outcomes and timelines. DBG also recommended:

> the establishment of Cabinet Sub-Committees for key areas of Government policy, the allocation of specific coordinating roles to Ministers and Ministers of State, the systematic sharing of expertise between departments, the development of project teams and the nomination of a 'lead Department' in each area to ensure that action is taken and the required outcomes achieved.

DBG recognised the need to set up structures and processes to develop and implement a change programme and to assign responsibility and authority to those who actually deliver the service. It promoted the publication of statements of strategy for each government department and office, but did not suggest any centralised monitoring of these against performance.

The PA Consulting Group's report (2002) acknowledges the benefits gained from the production of strategy statements and business plans, but comments unfavourably on the lack of central coordination, which reduces their value as a support to policy implementation. This leads to poor alignment between political intent, strategy and business planning and service delivery.

The PA report also comments on the variation in quality and usefulness of the annual reports when produced. The format of some annual reports did not correspond with the statement of strategy, making an assessment of progress very difficult. A review published in CPMR Discussion Paper 18 (Boyle, 2001) reveals that almost half of departments and offices failed to produce an annual report. The review was critical of the annual reports in existence and observed that 'In general, the reports do not provide a sufficiently balanced and informed picture of how departments and offices are progressing against agreed objectives and strategies.'

Today there is an increasing recognition of the need for some type of centralised or independent scrutiny to ensure delivery of policy. New initiatives are frequently accompanied by a monitoring and compliance system; for example, the provision of an Information Commissioner with the Freedom of Information Act 1997 and An Comisinéir Teanga with the Official Languages Act 2003. The latter's responsibilities include under section 21 (a): 'to monitor compliance by public bodies with the provisions of this Act'. The National Disability Authority is monitoring the implementation of the National Disability Strategy, formulated by the Cabinet Committee on Social Inclusion. The recent Social Partnership Agreement *Towards 2016* includes the mechanisms to ensure implementation. Among these are a steering group to take overall responsibility 'for the management of the implementation of the ten-year framework as it applies to the wider non-pay issues' and quarterly plenary meetings of the four social partner pillars, chaired by the secretary general of the Department of the Taoiseach, to review, monitor and report on progress.

The establishment of the Performance Verification Group (PVG) under *Sustaining Progress* (2003) introduced a new review mechanism for the Civil Service. Boyle (2006), in his review of the PVG, concludes that the process 'has had a positive impact on industrial relations stability, co-operation with flexibility and change, and implementation of the public service modernisation agenda'. However, he also comments on the limitations of the procedure, particularly in relation to the limited scope of the modernisation agenda. For example, the PVG mandate does not include the monitoring of the quality of the PMDS, which is fundamental to improved performance and achievement of strategy. Discussions at the PMDS network suggest that department and agency engagement with PMDS varies from not doing any appraisals, to a tick-box exercise done by email, to the establishment of a committee to evaluate the quality of the process and ensure consistency across the organisation. Thus, managers taking the easy option of giving inappropriate or uniformly high grades may thwart the purpose of the linkage of PMDS with increments and promotion in 2007.

Boyle (2004) emphasises the importance of the centre's role in monitoring and evaluating progress with implementation of modernisation. He suggests that, 'the further development of progress reports to Civil Service PVG could be a positive development – particularly to improve the evidence base presented by departments and offices on the intermediate and final outcomes of modernisation initiatives.' The concept of the PVG being the oversight body for all implementation and progress reports has its attractions. However, Boyle warns that the 'over-identification of Civil Service modernisation with national agreements may run the danger of modernisation being subsumed into this particular industrial relations mechanism.'

Experience in other countries

The value of strong central government structures to implement policy has been recognised in many countries: Australia, New Zealand and the UK have explicitly highlighted the whole-of-government challenge. As the Australian report *Connecting Government: a Whole-of-Government Response to Australia's Priority Challenges* states: 'There is a need for careful choice of the appropriate structures to support whole-of-government work, and experience has shown that secretaries are often able to resolve the way forward on difficult whole-of-government issues more quickly and effectively than lower-level communities.'

Following recognition of the gap between cabinet decisions and effective implementation, Australia established the Cabinet Implementation Unit (CIU) in 2003 with the primary task of ensuring the committed and effective delivery of key government decisions. CIU activities fall into three main categories.

- It ensures that the cabinet has high-quality inform-ation on implementation issues by requesting a detailed implementation plan from the affected organisation(s). The plan shows how inputs and outputs are linked to policy objectives, describes assumptions, clarifies risks, and identifies tangible intermediate and long-term objectives.
- It monitors selected initiatives through quarterly reports to cabinet on the achievement of milestones and target dates and highlighting issues that need intervention.
- It promotes best practice in project management through guidance on individual implementation plans and identification and support of better practice principles.

The CIU uses a risk-based assessment to select the key initiatives for monitoring. At the time of our visit, it was monitoring 70 major initiatives involving up to 170 policy measures. We were informed that as a result of the CIU initiatives, larger agencies have established their own internal project offices to monitor the implementation of decisions, such that the report to the CIU is just the last link in a chain.

This sharper focus on implementation and delivery was demanded by Dr Peter Shergold, Secretary at the Department of the Prime Minister and Cabinet, when he stated in a 2004 speech: 'I want public servants with a fire in the belly about managing projects and delivering programmes on budget, on time, to the highest quality standards.' We learned that state governments in Queensland, Victoria and New South Wales have also established implementation units.

In the UK, perceived inadequacies in delivering joined-up government led to the establishment of the Prime Minister's Delivery Unit in 2001 with the objective of helping government to deliver better and more efficient public services. This unit works in tandem with the cabinet and Treasury to evaluate delivery and provide performance management for priority initiatives, and to assist departments in achieving their public service agreement targets. It accomplishes this through:

- partnership with departments to ensure a shared understanding of issues and a shared commitment to action
- engagement with people at all levels in the delivery system to understand the impact of the existing policy and the benefits and risks of the proposed action
- challenging departments on delivery planning and implementation outcomes
- close monitoring of progress against key policy targets.

New Zealand did not opt for a cabinet implementation unit. Instead, its 2001 *Review of the Centre* recommended a reporting system that put greater emphasis on accountability for outcomes and output specifications. The State Services Commission has an active role in monitoring the annual SOIs produced by the departments and agencies. This differs from the Irish process of formulating strategy statements in terms of the degree of scrutiny of the strategy for alignment with government policy, real performance indicators, relationship to outcomes, and the degree of accountability for achievement.

In addition to the SOIs, the New Zealand State Services Commission reviews and reports on the performance of public service chief executives. As the chief executives are on short-term contracts (maximum of five years), there is considerable pressure to perform. A number of high-level personnel we met believe that this has proved to be a mixed blessing. Critics such as Alex Matheson (2006) point out that the departmental CEOs tend to take a short-term perspective and often respond to this challenge by restructuring shortly after appointment. The resultant churning of staff, Matheson suggested, has been detrimental to long-term planning and staff development.

We are aware that the fragmented approach of the current implementation arrangements can cause coordination difficulties. The general issue of cross-service coordination and collaboration is addressed in the next section.

Cross-organisational structures for coordination and collaboration

The Irish experience

PA Consulting Group (2002) acknowledges the success of new cross-cutting structures in some policy areas (such as child welfare), but states that 'In relation to more routine instances of overlapping concerns across departments/ Offices we have seen less evidence of effective collaboration arrangements' and 'With some exceptions, progress on cross-cutting issues has been disappointing with the system still struggling to find practical collaborative mechanisms to progress the management of these issues.' Following a recommendation of PA Consulting Group, cabinet committees were established which have been successful in getting policy agreement on some contentious cross-departmental issues such as infrastructure, disability, health and decentralisation. Cabinet committees do not have a formal implementation role, although regular reporting to meetings has a positive impact on performance. In some cases other bodies have pursued implementation. As noted above, the National Disability Authority has a role in monitoring the implementation of the Disability Strategy within departments.

Committee for Public Management and Research (CPMR) discussion papers 4 and 8 (Boyle, 1997a, 1999) provide a valuable overview of the Irish experience in managing cross-cutting issues. Boyle (1999) highlights the importance of strategic results areas (SRAs) as a means of promoting a shared vision among different actors; the use of coordinating mechanisms such as regulatory, financial and communicative instruments (e.g. green papers) to steer initiatives, particularly in a network environment; the application of financial incentives such as joint budgets; the use of cross-cutting teams drawn from, but operationally detached from, the constituent organisations; and the establishment of cabinet sub-committees and the appointment of ministers for state to lead departments to coordinate actions.

Detailed recommendations for SRAs were also proposed by Whelan *et al.* (2003)[2] in their submission on cross-departmental challenges. They suggested that the cabinet, advised by the Secretaries General, should identify a few priorities in terms of whole-of-government issues. These priorities should cascade down the service and link into individual departments' strategy statements. Progress in achieving the SRAs should be scrutinised by a joint Oireachtas committee or an external expert task force with secretariat service from the Department of the Taoiseach.

Boyle (1997a) discusses the use of teams within the Irish Civil Service and identifies a number of types of team falling under broad category headings of temporary and permanent teams, including the following.

- *Task force*: temporary group brought together for a specific task that is non-routine. Task forces have a mix of autonomy and dependence and usually only make recommendations.
- *Quality improvement teams*: modelled on practice in private sector manufacturing and service industries, small teams identify problems in work processes and propose solutions to management. The teams, which can contain members from beyond the direct work area, often implement the solutions themselves and disband after the issue in question has been dealt with.
- *Cross-functional teams (CFTs)*: composed of persons from across organisations or between departments/ agencies that supplement normal structures. CFTs usually have broad mandates and often have multiple leaders. Senior management agree parameters of decision making.
- *Work teams*: permanent teams created to produce specific end-products and usually with a significant degree of

---

[2] A group of senior public servants who published a study on cross-cutting issues in the Irish public service.

autonomy and decision-making capability, e.g. valuation office.

- *Top management teams*: the departmental management advisory committee (MAC) is an example. Boyle and Worth-Butler (1999) describe the development of cross-functional teams in the Valuation Office and Coillte Teoranta, where the multi-stream structure was abolished. The paper considers the difficulties posed by operating in a multi-stream environment composed of administrative, professional and technical streams. The report acknowledges that multi-stream structures were widespread in the public service, and difficulties presented included separate senior management levels, non-participation in policy-making by professional and technical staff, slow and poor information exchange between streams leading to poor coordination across departments and agencies, the prevalence of different cultures and allegiances between the streams, and poor promotion and mobility opportunities for professional and technical staff. In general, Boyle and Worth-Butler noted that while there was evidence of localised efforts to improve coordination and communication, there was little evidence of a systemic approach to addressing a problem that had been highlighted as far back as the Devlin report in 1969.

There may be many reasons for not tackling cross-departmental issues: for example, an organisation culture that encourages a narrow focus on work specifically within its remit without considering the needs of related service providers or opportunities for synergy; or a lack of incentives or acknowledgement for external achievements. In any case, deficiencies in mechanisms for dealing with cross-service issues have been ameliorated to some extent by both formal and informal networks.

Networks in the Irish public sector

Networks are another way of enhancing coordination in the complex environment of the public sector. They are characterised by the exchange or sharing of resources between organisations to achieve objectives; the common interests of the participants are greater than their differences, hierarchy is replaced by reciprocity and bargaining, and each organisation retains its autonomy. According to Kanter (1990), the characteristics of successful networks are based around eight 'I's: *importance* and *individual* excellence, where all the partners are strong and have something significant to achieve through *interdependence*, are prepared to *invest* resources, *institutionalise* the decision processes and role responsibilities, develop *integration* and have open *information* and full *integrity*.

Networks in the Irish public sector fall into three main categories, as follows.

- *Intra-departmental networks*: Some departments lead regular network meetings of their agencies or associated offices. These enhance communication and enable collaboration on issues of mutual interest and interdependence.
- *Interdepartmental and agency networks*: The Centre for Management and Organisation Development in the Department of Finance leads some very useful networks such as the PMDS and training officers' and personnel officers' networks. Participants in these have benefited from the sharing of information and experiences, identifying the information deficits and organising updates and speakers. The Change Management Network was established by the Implementation Group of Secretaries General to assist and support the integration of the modernisation process in departments and offices.
- *Informal networks*: These are the most vital networks in any organisation (Pettigrew *et al.*, 1992) and are essential in the vast complexity of the public sector. Fortunately, natural Irish gregariousness often helps to maintain the contacts made informally. Departments can nourish informal networking by encouraging social events and initiating meetings of staff from different units.

Lawton (1999) warns of the danger of underestimating the difficulties in successfully maintaining more formal networks. Success depends on the clarification of the purpose of the networks and the identification of the joint goals and expectations of the participants. Gould and Campbell (2002) point out the importance of the 'parenting' role in sorting out contentious issues and setting clear accountability parameters. It can be argued that this role is absent from parts of the Civil Service, and difficulties are allowed to continue without any real accountability for the lack of progress.

In conclusion, although networks have contributed to coordination and collaboration in the Irish public service, they are insufficient on their own – particularly for contentious issues – and do not replace a systemic approach to managing the implementation of cross-cutting issues.

Cross-organisational coordination structures outside Ireland

The Australian experience is that traditional interdepartmental committees are effective in the coordination of routine issues and for crisis management but are less successful for contentious issues and tight time limits. In the latter situations, the Australian public service chooses one of the following.

- *Task forces* are used to tackle issues with short time-lines and a clear objective, such as public sector reform, micro-economic reform, income security, and pensions. Those participating are expected to leave their departmental interests behind to join a creative group focused on problem-solving and delivery.
- *Joint teams* are distinguished by having staff from two or more departments work together to deliver shared outcomes. The team has a lifespan of several years. No department has the lead role, and to the external world employees are identified as members of the joint team rather than from their department.
- *Frontier agencies* provide expertise, dispassionate advice and programme administration on complex issues. An example is the Australian Greenhouse Office, which works to two ministers (Environment; and Industry, Tourism and Resources) and engages with the interests of all sectors of the economy, states and regions, other

governments, multilateral international organisations and many nongovernmental organisations (NGOs). These agencies are used when issues are contentious across a range of stakeholders, the symbolism of a separate agency is important and multidisciplinary skills are needed for a number of agencies.

On our trip to Australia we also learned about coordinating practices at state level. For example, in New South Wales a committee of CEOs meets regularly to review progress on cross-cutting issues. There is also an arrangement whereby clusters of agencies work to address gaps in services, improve delivery, foster networking and cooperation, and improve the use of resources, and the clusters report to the CEOs. We understand that these arrangements work better in some cases than in others. The state of Victoria has recently introduced the concept of 'place-based management' for departmental secretaries. In addition to his or her normal portfolio, the secretary has responsibility for a particular geographic region within the state. Regional management fora also help build a whole-of-government view and facilitate the identification of shared priority issues.

At federal level in Australia the Cabinet Implementation Unit has an important coordinating role. For example, it allocates a lead agency when there is a cross-cutting issue and it follows up on agencies that are obstructing progress.

Following the recommendations in the *Review of the Centre* (2001), New Zealand developed a number of structures to overcome the problem of fragmentation and improve alignment. The *mandated network* leads the development of an 'all-of-government approach' to the economic and social development of a region. The mandate from ministers includes the development of a shared view of the priorities for central government intervention in the region and an agreed approach to address the identified priorities, improve coordination, and reduce overlaps and redundancies in government intervention.

The New Zealand Controller & Auditor General has identified key success factors for effective coordination between public sector agencies, including the following.

- Assignment of a lead agency.
- A regular forum to ensure continuing coordination of sector initiatives, work programmes and projects.
- A set of common outcome statements consistent with government goals and priorities and a joint framework for measuring achievements.
- Clear governance arrangements, with definition of roles and responsibilities of each agency in the group.
- Sector agencies should draw up sector-wide data-sharing arrangements.

When coordination is seen to fail and specific inter-agency operational issues arise, mechanisms such as *circuit breaking teams* have been used. These are front-line based, inter-agency teams that provide creative ways to solve problems that have proved intractable over time. These teams are effectively a hybrid version of the Australian task forces and joint teams.

The differences between Ireland and these countries would appear to lie not so much in the types of coordinating structures employed as in the high-level focus on significant cross-cutting issues and monitoring of their progress.

Conclusions and recommendations

The case for structural reform

Structural reform – described as 'the heavy machinery of reform' by the OECD (2005a) – is one of the key methods used in modernising governments. The outcome is very visible and leads to more rapid cultural change than any other reform mechanism. Structural reform is driven by the need to meet new demands for public services, by political response to public concerns, by decentralisation and specialisation, and by the need to develop better arrangements for policy coordination. By its nature, the conventional Civil Service machine bureaucracy is constrained in terms of flexibility and responsiveness. The first objective of most structural reform is therefore to free delivery organisations from the constraints of the traditional Civil Service, making them more responsive to customer requirements. The second objective is to introduce competition into service delivery, making it more efficient. Such reform is normally external, involving the creation of agencies or the use of market mechanisms. The negative impact of such reform lies in the areas of control, coordination and accountability. These are addressed by way of further internal structural reform at the centre of the Civil Service, allowing for new mechanisms and procedures for dealing with these specific issues.

Department–agency relationships

Ireland has pursued a substantial agencification programme over the past 20 years. This has occurred in the absence of any formal framework, leading to variety in terms of size, legal basis, operation and accountability of the agencies created. There has been inevitable overlap or duplication of functions. There is no formal system of review to assess the performance of – and indeed the continued need for – the agencies. The benefits of this reform are therefore difficult to assess.

We believe there is a need to bring greater coherence to the roles, operation and governance of existing agencies in Ireland today. This would be facilitated by the following measures.

- A formal framework for the establishment and operation of agencies needs to be developed on the lines proposed by Prospectus (2003) for the health services in other key sectors characterised by multiple agency arrangements.
- The remits of agencies operating within such frameworks should be refocused to take account of whole-of-government objectives.
- Periodic (say five-yearly) reviews should be undertaken of each agency within the framework for continued relevance and performance. This review would complement ongoing corporate governance arrangements. It would also be appropriate when establishing new agencies in the

future to set this periodic review process within the context of a 'sunset clause' in the agency service-level agreement or memorandum of understanding to underline the significance of this review.

- The benefits of adopting an executive office approach over the more commonly pursued agency route merit serious examination, particularly in the light of the findings of McGauran *et al.* (2005) in relation to the large number of small, fragmented public bodies and agencies in Ireland today. Such a review should also have regard to experience of the executive agency model introduced under the UK *Next Steps* (1988) framework.

The governance challenge

Effective agency governance arrangements in departments are critical to promote strong agency performance and accountability. There also needs to be a sound legal and institutional framework that both provides a clear operational framework and acts to limit the number of bodies created.

The development of departmental capacities to undertake the governance role should be given high priority. This might best be done through departments with a number of agencies cooperating in a cross-departmental review to establish best practice.

The level of central governance applying to Ireland's 600+ agencies varies widely. There is a general need for improved and consistent governance arrangements. This should be addressed in a way that does not undermine the requirement for operational freedom that led to the creation of agencies in the first instance. The following measures are proposed.

- The appropriateness and value of having officials on agency boards, and their role and circumstances, should be reviewed to facilitate policy alignment and agency delivery, as recommended by McGauran *et al.* (2005).
- In parallel there should also be development of departmental capacities to undertake the governance role. Departments with a number of agencies should cooperate in a cross-departmental review to establish best practice.

This review should also address the value of establishing separate governance units versus maintaining the responsibility within line units.

Policy alignment/coordination and subordination

Government policy must be aligned between the centre and the periphery irrespective of what delivery mechanisms are in operation. This requires coordination at all levels in regard to development, implementation and subsequent monitoring. To enhance this area of performance between departments and agencies:

- consideration should be given to the introduction of a pre-policy audit process, similar to that pertaining in New Zealand
- periodic structured meetings should be held between agency chairpersons, their CEOs and department heads.

Securing agency performance

Securing improved agency performance is essential to the challenge of better public services delivery. At the heart of this is improved monitoring and evaluation of agency performance through the application of an appropriate performance indicator framework. Such a framework needs to be developed for each body linked to the service planning and budgetary processes.

The performance measures should also include a whole-of-sector perspective. To facilitate this, agency SLAs and MOUs should include specific obligations in relation to data sharing and reporting, and performance assessment should include reference to the contribution of these elements to whole-of-sector goals.

Transparency is also an essential element in securing agency performance. Agency assessments, in line with the government's new expenditure review arrangements, should be published.

Market mechanisms

The use of market mechanisms to improve performance and delivery is increasing in OECD member countries. There is substantial evidence to support the general tenet behind marketisation in terms of reduced costs and better services. However, these do not flow automatically. Mistakes have been made and important lessons learned. The Irish marketisation programme must take account of this.

Public–private partnerships (PPPs)

As noted above, PPPs are arrangements whereby the private sector designs, builds, finances, maintains and operates infrastructural assets. While the philosophy underlying this approach has merit, the outcomes have not fully matched expectations. Initial PPPs were not particularly successful and became advantageous only after the process was subjected to detailed scrutiny and development. We believe, therefore, that the use of PPPs needs to be kept under review.

Outsourcing

A national policy framework for the application and implementation of outsourcing should be developed along the lines of that applying for PPPs.

For many specialist services provided through either PPPs or outsourcing there is often a need to retain some public sector capacity. This is critical in regard to the provision of the necessary supervision and governance arrangements. It provides contingency in regard to high-skilled strategic areas, provides benchmarking and promotes competition.

Vouchers

We believe that it would be beneficial to consider the potential for wider application of voucher mechanisms in Ireland as a means of achieving improved service delivery targeting, to provide greater choice to service recipients. A policy framework for the appropriate use of these market mechanisms should be developed, having regard to experience here and abroad to date.

Reform at the centre: structures for implementation and monitoring

The structural changes under the modernisation agenda have given rise, *inter alia*, to agencification and, in some areas, the removal of service delivery as a primary role for the core Civil Service. This has caused silos to develop due to the policy–operations split and the consequent lack of coordination among institutions. The new role for the centre requires both a greater capacity to monitor and assist the implementation of the various change initiatives and subsequently the provision of better mechanisms to provide for coordination between the decentralised bodies and the centre.

The experiences in Ireland and other countries described above suggest that successful implementation is usually linked to some type of body or bodies with a review and monitoring role. These bodies perform one or more of the following functions:

- review of strategy plans to ensure they are in line with government policy and contain appropriate performance indicators
- evaluation of what has been achieved relative to the performance indicators and spending
- ensuring that high-priority policies are implemented through ongoing monitoring of progress, identification of obstacles and interventions to remove them.

In Ireland these functions are performed to some extent, either directly or indirectly, by a combination of the PVG, cabinet committees and the Comptroller and Auditor General (C&AG). In Chapter 4, we explore the effect of public accountability arrangements on performance and delivery and the possible future role of the C&AG in the evaluation of outputs and outcomes linked to financial reports.

The effectiveness of the PVG in delivering whole-of-government policies has yet to be established. In its second phase under *Towards 2016* the PVG may take a stronger stance in relation to performance, but it is likely to remain hampered by the vagueness of negotiated agreements designed to satisfy different bodies in the discussions.

Furthermore, for practical and political reasons, linking all assessment of performance with the partnership process (as observed by Boyle) may not be the best way forward. Therefore, we consider other options to ensure the implementation of high-priority policies.

The original Coordination Group of Secretaries General, comprising a sub-group of Secretaries General, successfully produced *Delivering Better Government* and the modernisation changes that followed. However, there is a view that the current Implementation Group of Secretaries General, which consists of all Secretaries General, is not as successful. In his discussion on the role of the centre in promoting modernisation, Boyle (2004) makes the point that 'the SMI Implementation group, whilst serving a useful function, is not an effective review body. It is seen as too big and more focused on steering/information exchanges.' Given the success of the original Co-ordination Group of Secretaries, the possibility of re-establishing a sub-group of Secretaries General with a clear remit could be explored.

An alternative to this approach is the establishment of a unit within the Department of the Taoiseach linked closely to the Department of Finance for overseeing policy implementation and whole-of government coordination to facilitate association of departmental assessments with budget allocations. This type of unit would be similar to the Cabinet Implementation Unit in Australia and the UK Prime Minister's Delivery Unit in that it would have responsibility for overseeing the implementation of high-priority initiatives.

In complex delivery situations, and particularly for major new initiatives where a number of actors are involved, the application of a formal implementation protocol would be helpful. This protocol would itself be subject to central review for effectiveness.

Implementation and monitoring

Responsibility for monitoring the implementation of major change in the public service rests directly or indirectly with a number of bodies such as the PVG, cabinet committees, the C&AG and the Implementation Group of Secretaries General. The approach is somewhat fragmented. Ideally we would favour the setting up of a professional implementation group along the lines of the Australian Central Implementation Unit or the UK Prime Minister's Delivery Unit. This would:

- have responsibility for overseeing the implementation of high-priority initiatives
- be located within the Department of the Taoiseach and linked closely to the Department of Finance in order to associate the departmental assessments with budget allocation
- possess the necessary expertise not just to monitor but to advise, assist and intervene where the implementation of high-priority initiatives was failing to meet targets.

Cross-organisational structures for coordination and collaboration

While development of a whole-of-government perspective is an essential factor for improved performance, progress in this area in Ireland has been poor in spite of numerous reports that highlight the deficiencies and suggest appropriate solutions. It is important to identify blockages that are inhibiting change in this area and to recognise the lack of incentive to compromise internally for the success of a cross-cutting initiative.

A multifaceted approach involving both structural and cultural change is required in order to make progress. On the structural front, we believe that the adoption of an approach similar to approaches in other jurisdictions, which involves the centre in identifying and monitoring strategic results areas, is called for now. An appropriate implementation monitoring group (e.g. PVG, CIU, cabinet committee, C&AG) should establish specific performance indicators to measure collaboration between organisations. These indicators should be chosen to eliminate duplication, discourage territorialism and encourage synergies between organisations. We agree with the proposal of Whelan *et al.* (2003) that progress should be evaluated by an external body such as an Oireachtas committee or an expert task force.

Changing structures alone will not produce the whole-of-government perspective required throughout the service. This perspective has to be encouraged and nourished through increased mobility between departments and agencies, measurement of an individual's contribution to cross-cutting issues, and making it a requirement for promotion to senior posts. The issues of lateral mobility and promotion of senior civil servants outside their original departments are addressed in Chapter 5.

4

Accountability for performance and delivery

In this chapter we look at the effect of public accountability arrangements on performance and delivery. We consider whether our current accountability arrangements need to change in order to promote a culture that values high performance and effective delivery. As indicated in Chapter 2, accountability systems, and the closely related issues of financial and performance management, are at the centre of much recent thinking and action on public service reform in other countries.

Our concern is with public accountability, meaning 'the obligation to present an account of, and answer for, the execution of responsibilities through the political and constitutional structure' (OECD, 2005a). In the course of the discussion we examine three aspects of accountability arrangements:

- the relationship between administrators and politicians
- the link between budgeting and performance
- reporting and auditing.

We begin with a brief exploration of the notion of account-ability and why it is important. We consider the changing nature of accountability systems in some other countries and outline the general principles underlying these changes, which are focused on accounting for performance.

We then look at the current accountability systems in Ireland, and in particular at the roles of ministers, Secretaries General and the Comptroller and Auditor General (C&AG), and identify some weaknesses from a performance and delivery perspective. As regards the relationship between administrators and politicians, the issue is summarised succinctly by Burgess *et al.* (2006):

> clarity in the accountability relationship at the top of the organisation is crucial. Ambiguity in the arrangements at the levels at which direction and strategy are set will reverberate throughout the organisation, sometimes with arbitrary decisions being taken at a lower level to compensate for lack of clarity above. These arbitrary actions can take organisations off course, contributing to a failure to meet objectives and produce intended results.

We go on to examine in more detail some key issues that will have to be addressed in any new, more effective accountability system, namely:

- budgeting for performance
- financial and non-financial reporting
- the role of national audit.

The link between budgeting and performance is vital because accountability for performance cannot be demanded realistically without reference to the resources available to achieve performance. It is for this reason that many jurisdictions are trying in one way or another to produce more performance information along with budget proposals.

Public reporting to stakeholders is also a key part of the accountability cycle. The trend is towards reporting that is geared to giving both financial and non-financial performance information. Meaningful financial performance reporting is difficult in the absence of accrual accounts; this in turn raises the question of whether some form of accrual budgeting is required.

Regardless of the accounting framework used, the auditor's role in relation to financial reporting is the same. However, issues arise in relation to the auditor's role in auditing performance information, the role of performance auditing and the auditor's role in promoting better administration.

Finally, we present our conclusions on accountability for performance and delivery based on the discussion in the earlier sections. We also offer some practical recommendations for progressing this important area.

Understanding accountability

What is meant by 'public accountability', and why is it important?

Accountability is a term that is often used in a very broad sense, but for the purposes of this chapter we adopt the rather narrow definition used by the OECD (see above).

While public sector organisations are ultimately accountable to the Oireachtas, in another sense they are 'accountable' to users of their services and to the public. They discharge this accountability by explaining their decisions and by publishing information about their activities that will enable members of the public to see how they have used their resources and discharged their responsibilities. Members of the public can also use mechanisms and channels such as parliamentary questions, referrals to the Ombudsman, FOI or the media to force accountability. This type of episodic accountability can be very important in influencing the behaviour of public bodies. However, formal public accountability to parliament is a cornerstone of the system, making it possible to call to account in a democratic way those holding public office. Thus, the focus of the present chapter is on the formal public accountability mechanism.

Before we consider the adequacy of current accountability arrangements, a fundamental question that must be answered is why public accountability is important in a constitutional democratic state. Aucoin & Heintzman (2000) answer this by proposing that public accountability serves three purposes:

- to provide a democratic means to monitor and control government conduct
- to prevent the development of concentrations of power
- to enhance the learning capacity and effectiveness of public administration.

The Auditor General of Canada (2002) identified three similar purposes served by accountability arrangements within Westminster-style government administrations:

- to control against the abuse or misuse of power
- to provide assurance that activities were carried out as intended and with due regard for fairness, propriety and good stewardship
- to encourage improved performance of programmes and policies, through reporting on and learning from what works and what does not.

Bovens (2005) has pointed out that behind these three purposes lies a far bigger, more abstract concern of public accountability. Ultimately, public accountability can help to ensure that the legitimacy of the public administration remains intact or is increased.

The changing nature of accountability and control mechanisms

The trend from ex ante to ex post control

As outlined in Chapter 2, the OECD (2005a) has identified a trend towards changing accountability and control systems that has taken place as part of the New Public Management (NPM) movement. The traditional systems of control in OECD countries, including Ireland, have focused on ensuring that funds are properly accounted for and regulations complied with. Such a focus is not entirely compatible with the NPM vision of a more flexible system where managers are given the scope to achieve wider goals within new and more fluid organisational forms, as discussed in Chapter 3.

According to the OECD, there is a move from *ex ante* to *ex post* control, and the development of stronger processes of internal control. Simply put, the *ex ante* to *ex post* trend is from a system where transactions (payments) were approved prior to commitment from a controller outside the spending ministry to one where internal management makes many financial and non-financial resource allocation decisions that are externally checked after the event.

Performance management

The context for the shift in control noted above is the emphasis on performance management, which the OECD (2005a) defines as 'a management cycle under which programme performance objectives and targets are determined, managers have flexibility to achieve them, actual performance is measured and reported, and this information feeds into decisions about programme funding, design, operations and rewards or penalties.'

Although various interpretations of performance budgeting and management exist, the OECD (2005a) reports a common trend of governments seeking to adopt a results-based approach to both management and budgeting that shifts budgeting, management and accountability away from inputs towards a focus on measurable results.

As the OECD (2005a) has pointed out, performance is only one dimension of accountability. Other aspects include ensuring that correct administrative procedures have been followed and that funds have been spent as allocated. The challenge is to find the right mix of accountability and control so as to avoid the danger that the new demands imposed by accountability for performance might overburden the system.

A new public accountability cycle?

Principles for effective accountability in the modern Civil Service

The Auditor General of Canada (2002), in a carefully considered examination of the requirements for modernising accountability arrangements in the Civil Service, suggested five principles that must underpin the new accountability systems if they are to be effective, as follows.

- *Clear roles and responsibilities*: the roles and responsibilities of the parties in the accountability relationship should be well understood and agreed upon.
- *Clear performance expectations*: the objectives pursued, the accomplishments expected, and the operating constraints to be respected (including means used) should be explicit, understood and agreed upon.

- *Balanced expectations and capacities*: performance expectations should be clearly linked to and balanced with each party's capacity (authorities, skills and resources) to deliver.
- *Credible reporting*: credible and timely information should be reported to demonstrate what has been achieved, whether the means used were appropriate, and what has been learned.
- *Reasonable review and adjustment*: fair and informed review and feedback on performance should be carried out by the parties, achievements and difficulties recognised, appropriate corrections made, and appropriate consequences for individuals carried out.

The Canadian report emphasises that it is not possible to design a 'one size fits all' accountability system. However, while the practice of these principles needs to be tailored to each accountability relationship, it suggests that the stronger the application of these principles, the more effective accountability will be.

New accountability system in practice

In practice, the new public accountability arrangements tend to follow a cycle that begins with the presentation of the budget estimates. These are accompanied by a substantial amount of information on plans, strategies and objectives. Depending on the jurisdiction, the information presented at this stage may be linked to either outputs or outcomes, or both. The non-financial information is presented in such a way as to facilitate future reporting of performance against plans.

After the year-end, the department reports on its financial performance by way of a set of accrual financial statements. Performance in terms of service achievements or outcomes is usually reported in an annual report. This is related back to the non-financial information presented with the budget estimates. There are usually fairly strict guidelines on what the annual report must contain. In some jurisdictions, the performance reporting and financial reporting are combined in a single document.

In Australia, the appropriations are made on the basis of planned outcomes set out in the Appropriation Bill. Agencies then identify outputs and administered items (services that agencies deliver but do not control) that contribute to the specified outcomes. An annual report on performance against targets, including the accruals-based financial statement of the agency, is presented to the relevant minister and tabled in parliament, where it is considered by the committee that oversees the agency's estimates. In addition, reports by the Auditor General on the financial statements of agencies are considered by the Joint Committee on Public Accounts and Audit, which also conducts inquiries into issues of economy, efficiency and the administrative effectiveness of agencies.

In New Zealand, each department or agency publishes an annual statement of intent (SOI) setting out performance expectations for the financial year. Chief executives sign output plans containing key output priorities linked to what is proposed in the SOI. The Estimates explain how the outputs are linked to the outcomes sought in broader government goals. The annual report of the agency reports against the forecast financial and service performance information in the SOIs and, as in Australia, the select committee that deals with the related Estimate considers this. A significant aspect of the New Zealand system is that the parliamentary committee examining the annual report and estimates receives independent advice from the Auditor General when it is doing so.

The UK framework has two main elements: public service agreements (PSAs) and service delivery agreements (SDAs). The former sets out the overall aim of a department with outcome targets, while output and process targets are specified in the latter. Ellis and Mitchell (2002) note that 'if PSAs are intended to answer the "what" question about public service commitments, the SDAs are intended to answer the "how" question.' The Treasury collects information on performance against targets every quarter and presents it to a cabinet committee that also deals with budget allocations. In contrast to Australia and New Zealand, the annual reports are not considered formally by parliament, although reports by the C&AG on the annual accounts of departments are considered by the Public Accounts Committee.

Conclusion

In a number of developed countries (the above three are merely examples of a wider phenomenon) there has been a move to performance-based budgeting. The principles underlying this change focus on clarity of responsibilities and expectations along with reasonable review of performance. These new systems move away from input-based funding to the allocation of public funds on the basis of outputs to be delivered in pursuit of defined outcomes. Performance against the targets determined in this process is usually assessed by some element of the political system when the following year's estimate is being determined.

It is important to note that failure to meet specific targets does not, in the cases we examined, lead to any automatic impact on subsequent years' allocations but is considered by the committee (of parliament or cabinet) examining the estimate. This should not be seen as a weakness in such systems, since it is not at all obvious that the correct response to the failure to meet performance targets is a cut in funding.

Despite the strong trend towards this approach internationally, the OECD (2004) has concluded that the 'jury is still out' on whether these systems are successful. However, from our examination of the literature and contact with officials in these countries, we conclude that they are sufficiently flexible to be workable while at the same time putting much greater emphasis on performance and delivery than the traditional input-based systems, which emphasise compliance with expenditure rules.

The accountability cycle in Ireland

There are, in effect, two separate cycles of accountability in operation in this country. Firstly, we have one based on the Annual Estimates, the Budget, the annual Appropriation

Account, audit by the Comptroller and Auditor General and consideration by the Public Accounts Committee. Secondly, there is the Statement of Strategy/Annual Report cycle.

The Public Service Management Act, 1997 requires the preparation of strategy statements by Secretaries General in which they specify the key objectives, outputs and related strategies (including the use of resources) to be pursued by the department. The strategy statement must be approved by the relevant minister, who arranges for it to be laid before the Oireachtas. There is also a requirement to prepare progress (annual) reports on its implementation. 'The objective in building the concept of outputs into the departmental Strategy Statement and in making them subject to consideration by Oireachtas Committees was to broaden the scope of accountability beyond the focus on inputs to include a greater emphasis on the outputs and performance of public services' (Mullarkey, 2002). This will be taken a step further with the production by ministers of the annual output statements from 2007.

The roles of minister and secretary general

If one of the five principles of effective accountability is clarity about roles and responsibilities, how clear are the respective roles of the minister and secretary general and the relationship between them?

Ministerial accountability

The role and status of ministers in relation to departments and their responsibility to Dáil Éireann are set out in the Constitution and in the Ministers and Secretaries Act, 1924. Murphy (2005) has pointed that there are two separate and distinct types of ministerial responsibility – legal responsibility and political responsibility. Individual ministers are legally responsible to the courts for the performance of the functions of the departments for which they have charge. The minister is, in a corporate sense, legally responsible for the official actions of each and every employee, even though he or she may not have been aware of those actions and may not have specifically delegated the function concerned – a legal principle often referred to as the 'Carltona doctrine'.

Political responsibility is provided for in Article 28.4.2 of the Constitution, which stipulates that members of the government are collectively responsible to Dáil Éireann for departments of state administered by them. Ministers have a duty to inform and explain actions to the Oireachtas, through such means as parliamentary questions. As such, they retain the prime democratic accountability for actions in areas under their supervision.

Managerial accountability

The legal basis for managerial accountability – which centres on the direct accountability of departmental officials to the minister – is the Public Service Management Act, 1997. The Act provides that the secretary general is responsible for managing the department and is accountable to the minister for so doing. The secretary general can delegate functions to another officer, who then becomes accountable to the secretary general.

Secretaries General, in common with other senior officials, may be required to appear before Oireachtas Committees on a variety of issues relevant to the department, including departmental strategy statements. The capacity in which Secretaries General (or other civil servants) appear before Oireachtas Committees (other than as accounting officers before the Public Accounts Committee (PAC)) is on behalf of the minister as part of the minister's constitutional responsibility. Reflecting the different responsibilities of ministers and civil servants, there is a statutory prohibition on civil servants expressing an opinion on the merits or otherwise of the objectives of a particular policy.

Role of Accounting Officer

A secretary general has a separate role as Accounting Officer. The responsibilities of an Accounting Officer can be summarised as:

- preparing the annual appropriation account for each vote under his/her charge
- ensuring the regularity and propriety of transactions for which s/he is responsible
- securing economy and efficiency in the use of resources
- establishing management systems used to evaluate effectiveness.

Accountability in respect of these matters is discharged through the preparation of the annual Appropriation Account and giving evidence before the Dáil's PAC. It is important to note that these responsibilities are personal to the Accounting Officer. In discharging them, the Accounting Officer is acting in a personal capacity and not as an agent of the minister.

Accountability of executive agencies

The move to devolve functions to executive agencies, as outlined in Chapter 3, also has implications for governance and accountability. It could be argued that such changes can lead to a democratic deficit in that ministers can avoid political accountability by indicating that an issue is an operational one and, therefore, is for the agency to deal with. The contrary view is that accountability can be enhanced by the formal delegation of responsibility to agency boards and chief executives, as this makes the relationship between the minister and the board/chief executive clearer and more transparent.

The legislation providing for the setting up of many of these newer agencies clearly delineates the respective roles of the agency and the minister and specifically provides for how the agency will be accountable to the minister and to the Oireachtas. However, this is not the case in respect of some of the older agencies, and this highlights the need for a consistency of approach across all agencies.

The challenge of achieving an appropriate balance between independence and accountability is arguably more difficult when one is dealing with regulatory agencies. Issues have arisen in the past in relation to the level of accountability of these agencies to the Oireachtas, in particular. However, a government white paper, *Regulating Better* (2004), proposed that systematic reviews would be carried out of the regulation of key areas and sectors, which will involve the review of the regulatory institutions in place. Such reviews will be governed by the six principles of good regulation identified in the white paper, one of which deals with the accountability issue by requiring that the body of regulation governing each area make it absolutely clear who is responsible to whom and for what.

Issues arising in relation to accountability changes

There has been some debate, both here and in the UK, on the continued relevance of the current approach to ministerial responsibility. Notwithstanding the fact that the 1997 Act did not seek to diminish the constitutional and statutory role and responsibility of ministers as explained by Murphy (see above), there has been a noticeable shift in attitude, on the part of ministers in particular, as to what level of responsibility they ought to assume for failures or shortcomings in their departments. This has implications for the exercise of accountability in the Civil Service.

Some commentators have expressed concern about this change of attitude (Murphy, 2005), and unease has been felt at senior management level in the Civil Service. In taking issue with the Joint Oireachtas Committee on Health and Children's comments on ministerial accountability in its report on the matter of long-stay residents in public and other residential facilities being wrongly charged, Murphy states in unequivocal terms:

> Clearly, the Government cannot be held responsible for the actions or inactions of individual civil servants of which they are not aware but corporate failures … are clearly the collective responsibility of Government … In addition, because Ministers relate to the Dáil in the normal course on all matters concerning their departments a clear convention has developed over time of individ-

ual ministerial responsibility for the administration of their particular department. Nevertheless, failure by the Government to consider its responsibility where serious and protracted illegality by a department has taken place is failure to perform its constitutional duty. Of course, acceptance by a Minister of responsibility does not absolve civil servants of their responsibility. But their responsibility is to the Minister and to the Government.

On the other side of the debate, the appropriateness of the current arrangements has been seriously questioned. Fine Gael and the Labour Party have recommended an overhaul of the current system, which would include:

- specifying the respective responsibilities of ministers and Secretaries General in statute in much greater detail than at present
- the abandonment of the Carltona doctrine and its replacement with a system that would permit ministers to delegate by written order specific powers to specific officers, who would be accountable within the department and also directly to the Oireachtas for the exercise of those powers.

Somewhat similar sentiments have been expressed in the UK. The Reform (2002) report, *Spending without Reform*, described the UK doctrine of ministerial accountability as an 'anachronistic fiction' and Rupert Darwall, the Director of Reform, said it essentially meant that ministers being accountable for everything were accountable for nothing.

Also in the UK, in proposing a reconstruction of constitutional accountability, Woodhouse (2000) suggests that the focus on where to lay the blame has resulted in ministers becoming too defensive and seeking to extricate themselves from anything that has happened in their departments:

Hence the need to move away from causal responsibility, with its emphasis on determining whether there has been direct ministerial involvement. This will not prevent the locating of blame in officials, which would seem unavoidable, and even desirable, as part of being forthcoming about what has happened. However, it should minimise the extent to which ministers seek unreasonably to locate culpability, particularly if officials were given the opportunity to defend themselves publicly against false or unfair accusations, something that they are at present denied.

If there were evidence of ministers moving from the traditional approach to ministerial responsibility in this country, perhaps a corollary of this would be to allow officials to speak publicly for themselves on their delegated responsibilities. This clearly would represent a fundamental change in the relationship between ministers and senior civil servants but perhaps the time has come when departmental officers, appearing before Oireachtas Committees for instance, should be allowed to speak on their own behalf for their delegated responsibilities. However, one would need to be mindful of the risk of everyone trying to evade responsibility in such a scenario.

This growing uncertainty and confusion about the respective accountabilities of ministers and senior civil servants is not helpful to the proper functioning of the Civil Service. What appears to be required is a fundamental re-examination of the relationship between ministers and senior officials.

Conclusions on the roles of minister and Secretary General

It is accepted internationally that accountability does not work unless the system facilitates the clear identification of the various players and their roles and then assigns responsibility. Because of the changing attitude to ministerial responsibility, it is vital that a clear and modern structure for ministerial and administrative accountability be provided in Ireland. It is only right that Secretaries General should be held accountable to their ministers for the efficient management of their departments. However, the requirement for an increased emphasis on the accountability of officials – within the departmental management structure and to the Oireachtas – must be in addition to, and not instead of, the accountability of ministers. Ministers' responsibilities and accountabilities must also be clearly delineated in law. At a minimum, ministers must be responsible and held account- able to the Oireachtas for ensuring that adequate standards are maintained in the performance of functions at official level.

What is required in the first instance is for ministers and senior civil servants to have an open and frank discussion on how best to delineate their respective responsibilities and accountabilities. Such a discussion should involve consider- ation of the issues raised above. A restructuring of this pivotal relationship should perhaps be in line with the five principles for effective accountability in the modern Civil Service suggested by the Auditor General of Canada (2002). This could be achieved, for instance, by the development of the statement of strategy as a contractual document between the minister and the secretary general along the lines of the performance agreements in use in New Zealand. A better definition of the relationships between ministers and senior civil servants would lead to a better working relationship and the maintenance of trust and confidence between them. It would facilitate the identification and development of the required skills and capabilities for senior Civil Servants. It would also lead to an enhanced accountability framework, to increased managerial flexibility and to improved perform- ance and responsiveness, to which politicians and civil servants alike aspire.

Role of the Comptroller and Auditor General in Ireland

The role of audit in an accountability relationship is often described as being to attest, i.e. to give independent assurance that the account being rendered can be relied upon. The value of such a role ought not to be underestimated. As the OECD (2005a) has pointed out, without good control systems – which include an independent assurance system – accountability is impaired, as claims to compliance and performance are unsubstantiated for outside observers who lack the knowledge to judge the character, veracity and reliability of the actors involved. An attest function is essentially neutral. It does not set out to prove the account wrong or to find fault with the actions of the person rendering the account.

In Ireland, the Comptroller and Auditor General (C&AG) is a constitutional officer charged with auditing the accounts of moneys administered by the Oireachtas – i.e. the Central Fund and moneys voted by the Dáil. In addition, he audits many non-commercial public entities under statute.

As well as carrying out a financial audit, the C&AG is required under Section 3 (10) of the Comptroller and Auditor General (Amendment) Act, 1993 to report on 'such matters as he considers it appropriate to report on arising from the audits carried out by him of the appropriation accounts …'. In deciding what matters ought to be reported, the C&AG takes account of special considerations that apply to the management of public organisations, such as the need for public business to be properly conducted (e.g. with due regard to propriety in awarding contracts or engaging staff) and the need to avoid waste and extravagance.

It is clear from the legislation governing his functions that the C&AG's audit responsibility in relation to the appropriation accounts goes beyond attest and includes reporting to the Oireachtas deficiencies he has identified in the course of his audit. Inevitably, this tends to give a negative tone to his reports.

The C&AG functions as part of a cycle of accountability. Once public money has been spent by a central government body, the C&AG is free to report to the Oireachtas on the regularity, propriety and value for money with which this has been done. The Committee of Public Accounts can take evidence on this report from the relevant accounting officer and can then issue its own report making recommendations to which the Minister for Finance must respond.

Evaluating the current public accountability system

Bovens (2005) has proposed that a public accountability arrangement can be evaluated from three perspectives: democratic, constitutional and organisational learning (or 'cybernetic', to adopt his terminology).

The question central to the democratic perspective is whether the accountability arrangement adds to the possibilities open to voter, parliament or other representative bodies to control the executive power. From a constitutional perspective, the key question is whether the arrangement contributes to the prevention of corruption and the abuse of powers. The cybernetic perspective focuses on the question of whether the arrangement enhances the learning capacity and effectiveness of the public administration.

So how well do the current public accountability arrangements in Ireland score when examined from these three perspectives?

It can be argued that in the past they have worked well from a democratic perspective. A minister must answer parliamentary questions about the conduct of his/her department and appear before Oireachtas Committees. Civil servants must give evidence to Oireachtas Committees including the PAC.

A criticism that can be made is that the arrangements do not go far enough to overcome one of the principal/agent problems, i.e. that of information asymmetry. In reality Oireachtas members may have relatively little information about the functioning of departments. Evidence of this is the use of the Freedom of Information Act by opposition members to try to obtain information about the activities of departments, which they can then use to raise questions about government conduct. So there is a question as to how complete and relevant is the information given to the Oireachtas.

An emerging, and potentially critical, issue is the increasing questioning of the doctrine of ministerial responsibility, and the consequent uncertainty about precisely where responsibility lies when problems arise. This issue is fundamental to our accountability system.

The arrangements have been largely effective from a constitutional point of view. In particular, the roles of the C&AG and the PAC are important here. The PAC can examine an accounting officer in relation to issues of regularity and propriety. In the case of serious irregularity it can recommend to the Minister for Finance that expenditure be disallowed, in which case the matter would have to be brought before the Dáil to be regularised. In practice such instances are very rare. It must be said, however, that the media coverage of 'corruption' in public office, and the tone of some political debate, would suggest that this assessment might be regarded as too sanguine by some members of the public.

It is from the cybernetic, or organisational learning, perspective that the most obvious weaknesses are evident in our systems. There is little doubt that public sector agencies react to issues raised in the Oireachtas. In particular, the fact that the PAC can revisit an issue gives a powerful incentive to an accounting officer to deal with any issue raised before that committee. While this is highly effective in itself, it gives rise to a number of risks, and two in particular: the distortion of priorities and a focus on process rather than outcome.

The risk of distortion

A major weakness is that issues may receive time, attention and resources not because they are the most important or the most urgent but because they have the most visibility. Indeed, the information asymmetry referred to above means that it is almost inevitable that the current accountability arrangements will have little positive effect in terms of how organisations deal with important issues – particularly if they are complex.

Commenting on the very similar accounting officer/Public Accounts Committee arrangement in the United Kingdom, Lord Sharman (2001) stated that it had worked well for many years. He suggested that rigorous parliamentary scrutiny of public finances had played a significant part in ensuring low levels of fraud and corruption in central government. He took the view that the arrangements were a sound basis for building future changes designed to cope with changing circumstances.

In Ireland, some people believe that both the PAC and the reports of the C&AG on which the PAC's deliberations are based are overly critical. Such views are not unique to Ireland. Similar views were expressed to Lord Sharman, who did not appear to attach much weight to them.

Assessment of performance

A second key weakness is that there is no formal accountability mechanism in which performance is examined against pre-existing criteria. Instead, the accountability mechanism is concerned to a high degree with process. Indeed, issues such as regularity, propriety and economy can all be understood as process issues. Process is important and will remain important. A flexible and entrepreneurial public sector is desirable but the electorate is unlikely to accept, for example, that procedures designed to prevent corruption or cronyism in the award of public jobs or contracts should be set aside in the name of flexibility. The difficulty is that when accountability becomes associated almost entirely with compliance, the only incentive is to avoid sanction. The other side of the coin is that the accountability mechanism is perceived to discourage innovation. If innovation requires risk-taking, then a corollary is that some failures will occur. The present system almost guarantees that failure will result in criticism via the public accountability mechanism.

The new annual output statement, from 2007, may help to redress this by providing a basis for accountability for performance. The Minister for Finance has said: 'It is intended that this statement will allow the Oireachtas and the public to assess what is being targeted for delivery through public expenditure … This will represent an important development and will tackle the information deficit in this area' (Minister for Finance, 2006). It remains to be seen whether this will prove successful. Some of the issues that may arise can be discerned from the experience of other countries with performance budgeting (PB), and are discussed below.

A new approach to public accountability?

Is it possible to implement a system of accountability that encourages high performance? Experience in other countries suggests that it is certainly possible to structure accountability systems in ways that avoid the weaknesses in our own current arrangements and that broadly follow the five principles for effective accountability identified above.

Budgeting and performance

Performance budgeting – an old idea revisited

The PB systems being developed in other countries are generally associated with a broader set of reforms of the public sector through which 'managers are given flexibility in order to improve performance and are then held accountable for results measured in the form of outputs and outcomes' (OECD, 2005a). PB is intended to encourage and facilitate a more flexible and innovative public sector by loosening *ex ante* controls by the centre while increasing *ex post* accountability for results.

PB is not a new idea. Perhaps its most notable and ambitious previous incarnation was in the planning–programming budgeting systems (PPBSs) in the 1960s and 1970s. PPBSs, which developed in the USA, was 'an essentially engineering approach to budgeting, which has proved ineffective in the bear-pit of Congress' (Kane, 1993). Its lack of general success in the USA was matched by similar experiences in other countries including Ireland, where it was adopted with some enthusiasm and significant effort, but was abandoned within a very few years.

In 1981 the Irish government returned, in part, to this theme in its white paper *A Better Way to Plan the Nation's Finances*. This ushered in some important changes in government financial management. Most relevant to this discussion was the publication of comprehensive public expenditure programmes (CPEPs) in which estimates were presented by policy programme, with associated objectives and actions. The CPEPs were published separately to the normal estimates process and had no direct relationship to it. They provided a significant level of new information and were, at the time, widely welcomed by politicians and others for this reason. However, it appears that they had little real impact and they were first reduced in scope and then ceased publication in 1989.

The lack of success of these previous exercises, internationally and in Ireland, does not give much ground for optimism about the introduction of PB now. Yet there is a major resurgence in interest in this approach, driven by the commitment to a managerialist approach to the public sector encapsulated in the New Public Management (NPM) movement. Indeed, in the UK, Australia, New Zealand and a number of other countries, performance-based budgeting has been part of the landscape of reform for some years. The latest incarnation of PB appears to be working better than its predecessors, in part because it is less ambitious and rigid than PPBS and in part because the advances in ICT create far greater opportunities now for tracking expenditure and operational performance. Also important is the fact that in these countries the move to PB has been driven by strong political commitment, as part of an international wave of public service reform.

It is clear that internationally PB is back on the reform agenda despite the errors and failures of the past because it is recognized that the conventional budgetary process is woefully inadequate for any purpose other than the control of inputs and of annual cash expenditure. In particular, 'the merits or demerits of policy programmes and of their management are not visible in the formal budgetary process, and the process provides few formal incentives for performance, beyond negative controls on failure to meet the legality/administrative propriety criteria' (Kane, 1993). Traditional systems also are unsuited to the modern demands for flexibility and responsiveness that are key to the development of a public service geared towards performance and delivery: 'traditional public administrative systems were not designed to be flexible and adaptive in a modern society with customized services, the need for constant adaptation, pressure for efficiency and the increased use of private agents' (OECD, 2005a). The new wave of PB, therefore, is best understood as part of a broader effort to encourage what NESC termed 'democratic experimentalism' through which devolution of authority increases the scope for innovation by state agencies, but is matched by an increased demand for transparency and accountability for results.

Obstacles to PB

A fundamental question is whether there is really a demand from politicians for well-defined objectives and measured outcomes when making appropriations. The OECD (2004) says that 'politicians generally do not make much use of performance information. Some 72 per cent of OECD countries include non-financial performance data in the budget documentation presented to the legislature, but in only 19 per cent of countries do politicians in the legislature use this information in decision making.' The basis for the latter figure is not clear.

As against that, in Australia, for example, legislators have pointed out that senators often use annual reports during estimates hearings and that it is common practice for senators to use the reports for examination of ministers and their officials (Senate Employment, Workplace Relations and Education Committee, 2005). However, it is possible that the positive experience of Australia and the countries that have successfully adopted PB may be exceptional in this regard.

This issue is fundamental, as 'to ensure that performance-oriented budgeting and management achieves its objectives, its introduction requires not only changes in the behaviour of managers but also of the ministry of finance and politicians in the legislature and the executive, who all must use this performance information' (OECD, 2005a). PB, therefore, requires a 'whole-of-government approach' that understands public administration and governance as part of an interconnected whole. In 2002, PA Consulting Group noted the absence of such an approach as a key weakness in the SMI process in Ireland.

Even if there is the necessary engagement by the political system, PB still faces formidable obstacles of an operational nature in accurately capturing costs and meaningfully defining and measuring outputs and outcomes and relating them to the performance of specific organisational units. The countries that have engaged with this challenge are reporting success in terms of improved transparency and accountability and enhanced delivery of products and services (Chan *et al.*, 2002), but the OECD (2004) is more sceptical and suggests that it is too early to judge the impact of PB, which it says is 'very much in its infancy'. The available literature, as well as studies of the quality of performance data in Australia and the UK dealt with later in this chapter, suggests that even the most advanced countries do not feel that they yet have adequate systems for measuring performance. Moreover, it is also clear that the promise of increased devolution of resource control (and the flexibility and capacity for innovation that this allows) has not been fully achieved although progress has been made. This was also the impression gained from our study visit to Australia and New Zealand, where officials operating these systems, while largely positive in their assessment of them, were quick to acknowledge that they were far from perfect and in need of continued improvement despite the effort invested in them in recent years.

Where does Ireland stand?

Ireland's SMI initiative has largely followed the same thinking as the other NPM countries, albeit in a milder and more gradualist form, and it is leading to an emerging interest in PB. From 2007, ministers are required to prepare an annual output statement (AOS) for their departments, which is to be submitted to the relevant Dáil committee with the annual estimates. The AOS sets out the objectives for the current year and report, with effect from 2008, on the outturn for the previous year; it also sets out the cost and output information for each high-level programme within the department. This is potentially an important step towards PB.

In Ireland, for the past 10 years or so we have been putting in place many of the elements that are needed for PB of this type: objectives have been defined, output and outcome performance indicators have been stated and (less frequently) measured, and cost centres have been established within modern accounting systems capable of producing accruals-based information. The AOS will bring this another step forward, and importantly will test the appetite of the political system for this type of information.

However, in other respects Ireland is well behind the leaders in the field. We have made little progress on the publication of accrual accounting information (without which, arguably, the cost of programmes cannot be fully determined), some departments still publish strategy statements and annual reports that contain little in the way of hard performance information, there is no external validation of the performance information that is published, and the integration of financial and non-financial information is in its infancy and proving difficult. In addition, there is very little indication of engagement by the political system with the accountability processes that have been developed through SMI, or with the performance information that they have delivered to date.

For Ireland to move to PB successfully and meaningfully will require more than merely publishing an AOS for each department. It will necessitate a significant change in process and behaviour in both the political and administrative systems. The experience of other countries suggests that to create the conditions for a more flexible and innovative public service would require that PB be implemented within a broader framework of devolved, but not reduced, control of resources and a strong focus on results in both political debate and administrative oversight and audit systems.

Perhaps for this reason, NESC in 2002 stopped short of recommending a move to PB when it examined these issues. But it called for 'a balanced approach to outputs, outcomes and inputs' and stressed the need to develop accountability for results through Oireachtas committees and to strengthen the links between evaluation and resource allocation. The new AOS is broadly in line with this approach and indeed goes somewhat beyond the NESC proposals, reflecting perhaps some progress on these issues in recent years.

Conclusions on budgeting and performance

PB is an important element in the overall programme to forge new accountability systems that are more focused on performance and delivery. The experience of PB in other countries shows that it is both workable and positive, even if it has yet to live up to all its promise. However, the lack of success of similar initiatives in the past, and the challenges being encountered in other countries pursuing this path at present, would suggest that we should continue with a stepped approach to the development of PB in Ireland.

The implementation of the AOS, and the political reaction to it, will be a crucial next step. Successful PB has only been introduced in countries where it had strong political backing, and it remains to be seen whether this is the case in Ireland. Budgeting and performance measurement, the two core elements of PB, are central to the accountability relationship between the political system and the senior Civil Service, which, as discussed above, is itself the subject of much current debate in Ireland and abroad. The publication of the 2008 and subsequent AOSs, which will present information on performance in the previous year, will provide a unique opportunity to decide whether PB could contribute to a results-focused public sector and how this would fit within the political–administrative relationship as it is developing in Ireland.

In the meantime, two practical measures could be taken to improve the chances of a successful move to PB in Ireland.

- External validation of the targets and performance indicators (PIs) proposed by departments for their AOS would be in line with best practice internationally and would help to ensure that the information provided was the most meaningful and best available. This could add significantly to the credibility of the exercise and to improving the quality of PIs generally in departments and agencies.

Ultimately, PB can only be built on a sound foundation of performance measurement and reporting in departments and, while much progress has been made in recent years, it is clear that we have some way to go in this regard. This issue is further discussed in 'Reporting non-financial performance' below.

• It should also be recognised that a fundamental objective of PB is to allow greater managerial freedom and encouragement to innovation at departmental and agency level. The administrative budget system has moved the Irish Civil Service somewhat in this direction. Further progress on devolution of financial authority and responsibility could be made, within this system, if there were the will to do so. A significant change in practice in this direction would lend greater credibility to any subsequent move to PB and would prepare the ground at departmental level by encouraging the necessary management responsibility.

Reporting financial performance

Reporting financial performance in an accountability for results regime

A key issue to be considered in any move towards an accountability for results regime is how financial performance ought to be reported. This depends to some extent on what questions the financial statements are designed to answer. In the case of a not-for-profit public sector body there are probably two key questions: what resources were consumed, and whether operations were conducted within budget. The first of these can only be fully answered by reporting on an 'accruals' basis of accounting, which captures the financial effect of all transactions and events that occurred during the reporting period. This is required to measure accurately the resources made available and consumed in the achievement of any task or programme and therefore, arguably, is a necessity if we are to understand properly the 'capacities' that must balance performance expectations in an effective accountability system.

Australia, New Zealand and the United Kingdom have

moved to accrual accounting. There is no evidence of any debate within these administrations about the relative merits of accruals versus cash accounting, although they acknowledge the major effort and considerable up-skilling needed to introduce an accruals system.

On the other hand, there continues to be some debate academically about the merits of adopting accrual accounting in the public sector. For example, Carnegie (2004) has identified persistent criticisms of the move to accrual financial reporting in the local government sector in Australia by councillors and other ratepayers who complain that the information is too narrow, too complex and often bewildering.

Criticisms such as these are probably better seen not as criticisms of accrual accounting *per se* but more as expressions of concern about attempts to take an accounting framework developed for private sector entities and to apply it in the public sector. In may be that too little effort has been made to recognise the genuine differences between the private sector and the not-for-profit public sector, and not enough attention has been paid to the needs of users of public sector accounts.

In 2003, the Association of Chartered Certified Accountants (ACCA) appeared to acknowledge such concerns when it urged the Accounting Standards Board (ASB) in the UK to be cautious in asserting that the needs of public sector account users can be met merely by re-expressing and expanding the ASB's existing accounting principles – which have a very strong private sector bias – to make them applicable to public sector organisations.

The worldwide emphasis on accurate financial reporting on the basis of agreed accruals standards in the private sector is creating pressure for the public sector to follow suit, if only to be seen to deliver comparable transparency and, in the words of an Australian review of the reforms in that country, to 'put the public sector on a more businesslike footing' (Australian Public Service Commission, 2003). International accounting standards setters have made considerable efforts to develop public sector standards that follow the private sector standards very closely. In any move to accrual accounting there may be a temptation simply to accept these standards so as to lend credibility to the exercise. This might prove to be a serious mistake. It would be preferable to adopt the ACCA approach, analyse the needs of account users and, based on that analysis, adapt the international standards to meet the requirements of the users.

Other uses of accrual accounting

It has to be recognised that accrual accounting is potentially useful for purposes other than public reporting. One use is in the initial assessment of proposed programmes. For example, the Australian review comments that 'government budgetary deliberations can now be made in the knowledge of the full costs of proposals. While there is no doubt that cash considerations remain prominent, the availability of full accrual information assists decision-making' (Australian Public Service Commission, 2003).

It can also facilitate good financial management. However, what may not be widely appreciated is that to realise this benefit a significant change is needed in the degree of autonomy given to budget-holders and in the incentives to good financial management practices. The better information given by accrual accounting is of little value to managers and budget-holders if, in reality, they have little or no discretion in terms of how the budget can be spent.

Cash accounting and budgeting can create a range of perverse incentives, such as leasing instead of purchasing capital goods, often at a significantly greater financing rate than the cost of government debt, or spending the cash budget near year end to avoid losing it. Accrual accounting and budgeting can be used to eliminate these incentives and to create incentives to good financial management such as charging departments and agencies for the cost of capital tied up in their operations, thus giving an incentive to manage assets efficiently. Incentives of this kind are a feature of the UK system of resource accounting and budgeting.

On the other hand, the claims made for accrual accounting can be overstated. It probably has most to offer in departments or agencies with significant operations, where with the right incentives it could promote efficiencies. It would seem to have relatively little to offer a department that is mainly concerned with policy-making and that has little by way of operations.

The position in Ireland

In discussing the question of a move to accrual accounting by the Irish Civil Service, one should bear in mind that a significant part of the public sector already accounts on an accruals basis, namely the non-commercial state agencies. As a result, their accounts are certainly more understandable and more informative to anyone with even a moderate level of financial literacy than the accounts of a government department.

How much use funding departments actually make of these accounts is not clear. It seems that the accounts' primary purpose is seen as a discharge of public accountability as opposed to providing useful information to an important stakeholder. While it is difficult to form any definitive view on the matter, it would seem that the levels of financial literacy in many departments may not be sufficient for them to derive much value from the accruals information in the accounts.

It is also the case that funding departments often fund these agencies on a cash basis. In other words, the agencies are given a maximum cash budget for the year and the fact that they may spend an amount in excess of this (on an accruals basis) appears to attract no sanction as long as the cash budget is not exceeded. The reason why a department's primary or even sole concern is the cash budget allocated to the agency is that the department itself is funded on a cash basis and it is far more convenient to fund an agency on the same basis than attempt to give it an accrual budget. Funding an agency on a cash basis really means that the value of accrual accounting as a management tool is greatly weakened. The approach currently adopted by funding departments towards agencies provides a possible indication of what will happen if accrual accounting is introduced into government departments but without accrual budgeting. There is a serious danger that accrual accounting will simply become a technical exercise that will not, as it should, encourage a focus on achieving financial efficiencies.

Accruals in practice: health boards and the HSE

One exception to the approach generally adopted by departments to agencies as described above has been that of the Department of Health and Children and the Health Service Executive (HSE)/health boards. From 1996 to 2004, the department funded the health boards on an accruals basis, on foot of legislation that permitted the minister to set a maximum level of expenditure that a board was permitted to incur in delivering on its ministerially approved service plan for the year. Having set a level of expenditure, the department estimated the cash required during the year to pay for the part of the expenditure that fell due for payment in the year, and made provision for this in the relevant year's estimate. Expenditure incurred in one year but falling due for payment in the following year was provided for in the following year's estimate separately to the provision for that (following) year.

Without further research, it would be difficult to say what effects the accrual budgeting approach adopted by the department had in encouraging better financial management in the health boards. As indicated above, budgeting and accounting are only one aspect of the matter – other features of the system could easily provide incentives to perverse behaviour. What can be said, though, is that the system avoided the incentive to spend up to the cash limit that is a feature of the cash budgeting system. Indeed, it provided no perverse incentive to incur expenditure up to the maximum expenditure limit either, because the department allowed unspent budgets to be carried forward to the following year. It is also worth recording that, taking the period 1996 to 2004 as a whole, the health boards did not incur significant deficits – proof that a move to accrual budgeting need not be a risk to budget discipline.

Ironically, the abolition of the health boards and the establishment of the HSE in 2005 led to the dismantling of the budgeting framework described above. The HSE was given its own vote, which means that it has to submit its own cash-based appropriation account each year. Surprisingly, it is also required by legislation to produce an accrual set of financial statements, although the purpose these are meant to serve is not clear. All in all, it can be concluded from the HSE experience that, despite the investment in new accounting systems, a lack of belief in the value of accrual accounting remains – at least for budgeting and public reporting purposes. The reason for this is not clear, but lack of financial literacy is almost definitely a factor.

Conclusions on accrual accounting

A decisive switch to accruals budgeting would necessarily involve a major once-off step change. A crucial part of the preparation would be a substantial increase in formal accountancy skills in the Civil Service through internal skills development and direct recruitment. Skills are required for improved financial management, and to obtain maximum benefit from the accounts systems now being installed in departments – even without a move to accruals – this step, at least, should be taken. With the new accounts systems in place and an adequate skills base, a decision on whether to move to accruals should then be largely based on the response to the AOS. If that leads to a decision to move to full PB, then a move to accrual budgeting may well be justified, particularly if it is preceded by a more active devolution of financial authority, as suggested above.

An increase in skills at the middle ranks of the Civil Service will not in itself guarantee that a switch to accruals will yield benefits. A change of this order would require a very clear articulation of the case for accruals, so as to secure senior management backing across departments, and probably political sponsorship – both of which have been missing so far to some degree. The slow progress to date and the reversion to cash accounting for the HSE suggests, at a minimum, a lack of conviction as to the merits of the accruals concept. The present slow and tentative approach carries the risk that accrual accounting will end up as a technical exercise resulting in increased costs but without commensurate benefits.

Reporting on non-financial performance

What does 'performance' mean in the context of a public sector body? It seems to be generally accepted that what is really important is outcomes, i.e. impacts on society. Of course, what impacts are aimed for is ultimately a political choice – there is no one set of impacts that will win universal approval. So, in theory at least, the performance of a public agency ought to be measured in terms of its contribution to specific, politically defined outcomes.

A clear trend is discernible in Australia, New Zealand and the UK towards a focus on outcomes in public sector management. A big challenge here is the quality of information needed for outcome-focused management. Relevant information for this purpose is 'state indicators' (how the world is), 'effectiveness indicators' (how well an intervention worked), and 'risk indicators' (information on where to intervene). As is clear from the studies on data quality carried out in Australia and the UK and described below, obtaining reliable state indicators can prove difficult. It can be even harder to measure the effectiveness of a particular agency or programme. Notwithstanding these difficulties, it would seem that reporting performance in an accountability-for-results regime has to involve reporting progress on achieving pre-agreed outcomes as well as some indication of the agency's contribution to that progress.

Reporting non-financial performance is not just a question of deciding whether to report outputs or outcomes. There are also issues concerning the quality of the reporting – it must be 'credible' in order to meet one of the key principles for effective accountability identified above. There are indications that – even in Australia and the UK, where more emphasis is placed on reporting of non-financial performance – the quality of the reporting leaves something to be desired.

It is hardly surprising, therefore, to find that in Ireland, where the contents of annual reports are not mandated by legislation, the non-financial data is not externally validated and the reports are not scrutinised by the Oireachtas – the quality of the reporting has been the subject of persistent criticism. Boyle (2001, p. 32) found that, in general, the annual reports of government departments were poor in explicitly comparing actual with expected performance.

A study by Wall and Martin (2003) confirmed the unsatisfactory quality of the reporting. The study looked at the annual reports of a sample of public bodies, North and South, and found that the quality of reporting in the latter compared very unfavourably with the former. For example, the agencies of the various government departments in Northern Ireland disclosed comprehensive key performance indicator (KPI) information and all linked the indicators and measurements to predetermined strategic objectives and targets.

This was in contrast to the performance data provided by Irish government departments. This ranged from the occasional indicator to, in one case, a comprehensive set of KPIs linked to objectives and targets. However, even with those that reported on several performance areas and linked these to strategic objectives, but not to specified targets, the information was not always well laid out. For example, one department dedicated a whole section of the report to each strategic objective, but then the user had to search through often lengthy narrative to ascertain the achievements.

The study's criticisms were not confined to government departments. It concluded that the Irish semi-state organisations generally disclosed the least information, with over half providing only the occasional KPI and none providing a comprehensive linking of KPIs to either stated objectives or targets.

In practice, annual reports of government departments generally receive little attention from politicians or the media. In common with strategy statements, they are formally laid before the Oireachtas and circulated to relevant committees, but they are not subjected to examination and debate – parliamentary scrutiny of these documents is in practice almost non-existent.

The requirement to publish meaningful AOSs, to be published alongside the estimates and examined in Dáil Committee, from 2007 is therefore a significant challenge for many departments. The Taoiseach has asked the Implementation Group of Secretaries General to review PIs in the AOSs to ensure that they are appropriate and useful. This will be critical if the process is to move our budgeting and accountability systems to a more modern performance-focused basis. Even more ambitiously, he has asked that these PIs have a sufficient degree of consistency to allow aggregate indicators to be established 'which show the impact of total public spending and the degree of progress in achieving the strategic priorities of public policy as a whole' (An Taoiseach, 2006b).

It is clear that if this challenge is to be met, a very significant improvement will be required in the quality of non-financial performance reporting in the Civil Service and public service. This further underlines the case for external validation of the appropriateness and relevance of performance indicators and of the quality of information used in reporting on them – a point we return to below.

The role of national audit in an accountability-for-results regime

Two of the principles for effective accountability identified above are credible reporting and reasonable review. These are crucial elements of any performance management system, and it is no surprise to find them also identified as key elements in modern accountability systems that have improved performance and organisational learning among their main purposes. International experience suggests that National Audit Offices can play a major role in encouraging credible performance reporting and in providing reasonable review through at least three measures:

- validating organisations' performance-reporting systems and data

- identifying and promoting best practice
- directly undertaking performance audits.

Validating performance-reporting systems and data

Experience in the UK, Australia and New Zealand underlines the important role that national audit offices can play in validating performance systems and data and, therefore, in reinforcing their contribution to effective accountability. In the UK, the Sharman Report (2001) recommended that there be external validation of departmental information systems as a first step in a process towards validation of key published data. Lord Sharman commented that the move to regular performance reporting for departments was a very important step in improving accountability, but that there was general agreement that a good deal of work needed to be done in preparing for these developments. He accepted that there were already strong links between validation and audit work, and in order to ensure a cost-effective process, the C&AG and Audit Commission, as the auditors of the bodies generating much of the data, should be responsible for external validation in their respective areas.

Validating performance-reporting systems and data: UK

On foot of Sharman's recommendation, the National Audit Office (NAO) in the UK conducted a study of data quality in reports on departments' progress in meeting their main public service agreement (PSA) targets in 2004. The NAO commented that departments had made variable progress in establishing robust systems to collect and report data. It found that in about 20 per cent of cases departments were not collecting data for the measures specified in their technical notes at the time of the NAO's validation work. In about 30 per cent of cases the NAO said there were weaknesses that departments needed to address in order to reduce the risk of gaps or errors in reports in the future.

The NAO conducted a second validation exercise in 2005. This concluded that 77 per cent of the systems examined provided a 'broadly appropriate' basis for measuring progress, although in two-thirds of systems either there were some weaknesses or further disclosures in the performance reports were needed so that readers would understand the implications of the weaknesses. On a more optimistic note, the NAO stated that by the end of 2005 departments had already addressed weaknesses in 20 out of 46 systems reviewed in response to recommendations in its earlier report, demonstrating the scope for departments to tackle the weaknesses identified.

Validating performance-reporting systems and data: Australia

The Australian National Audit Office (ANAO) carried out a performance audit in 2003 designed to determine whether agencies had:

- established a sound annual reporting performance information framework
- developed arrangements to ensure that performance information is accurate and coherent
- appropriately analysed performance information in their annual reports.

The findings of this audit were very mixed. On the one hand, the ANAO concluded that outcomes, agency outputs and administered item outputs were well specified in most instances. On the other hand, it suggested that, in order to provide accountability and transparency to parliamentarians and other stakeholders, agencies' annual reporting frameworks needed to be improved, particularly in relation to:

- the specification of agencies' influence on, and contribution to, shared outcomes
- performance measures relating to quality and effectiveness/impact
- the efficiency of agency operations and the cost-effectiveness of outputs delivered
- targets or other bases for comparison.

The ANAO also concluded that performance information generally had not been presented and analysed in annual reports in a way that would allow parliamentarians and other stakeholders to interpret and fully understand results.

As regards data quality, the ANAO was able to conclude that agencies had developed arrangements to provide performance information that was accurate, coherent and consistent, but only in those areas of the annual reports examined in the course of the audit. However, it suggested that establishing and monitoring agency data quality standards, improvement in documentation of costing approaches, and a review by particular agencies of the correlation between their internal and external reporting frameworks would assist agencies to ensure that performance information in future annual reports would continue to be accurate, coherent and consistent.

Validating performance-reporting systems and data: New Zealand

In New Zealand, validation of performance reports has gone an important step further than in the UK and Australia. There the auditor is required to express an opinion on whether the financial statements – which include a 'statement of service performance' – fairly reflect the organisation's service performance achievements measured against the performance targets adopted for the year.

Officials in the Office of the Auditor General did not identify any particular problems in auditing this information and expressing an opinion. In part, this may be because the New Zealand system is fairly long established. It may also reflect the fact that the scope of performance reporting is less ambitious than, say, in the UK. The Auditor General (2005–2006 report, 7.27) has indicated that the audited financial statements almost exclusively contain output reporting. There is some outcome reporting but it is presented separately in the annual report and is not audited. The Auditor General has indicated that he expects the 'gradual' introduction of some outcome reporting into the audited financial statements. As of March 2006, his assessment was that there was not yet a demonstrable improvement in the quality of departmental performance reporting, which might have been expected as a positive effect of the quality of planning that the Management for Outcomes initiative promotes.

The role of national audit in promoting best practice

In an accountability regime that is focused more on performance, can the auditor's contribution go beyond giving assurance and extend to promoting better performance? An important consideration here is whether adopting such an approach will compromise the independence of the auditor by impairing objectivity.

Lord Sharman (2001) commented that external audit of public money is undertaken primarily from the perspective of the 'watchdog' – designed to provide assurance that taxpayers' money has been well spent – but to make the most of the work, auditors should seek to combine this role with that of adviser in ways that do not compromise independence.

The ANAO has adopted an approach to its role that fits, to some degree, with Lord Sharman's idea of how better use could be made of public audit to promote better performance. ANAO officials indicated that the role of the office had changed somewhat over the years. Originally, it had a traditional audit role that was focused on assurance. Now it defines its mandate in terms of two outcomes; namely, improvement in public administration and independent assurance of financial reporting, administration, control and accountability.

The officials indicated that the ANAO believes it can contribute to improvement in public administration while maintaining its independence and not becoming part of executive government. One vehicle for promoting improvement is a series of 'better practice guides' that draw lessons from audits. The emphasis is on better practice as opposed to 'best' practice, as the guides are not intended to be prescriptive. Also, more recently the office has taken a decision to produce only guides that are based on the findings of its audits – as opposed to, for example, research conducted by it or on its behalf. A second vehicle for promoting better administration, recently introduced, is a newsletter intended to bring lessons learned from audits to a wider public sector audience.

Performance audits

The OECD (2005a) has pointed out that 'performance' or 'value-for-money' (VFM) audits have been adopted almost universally by national auditors. A performance audit is generally concerned with issues of economy, efficiency and effectiveness; the precise scope depends, to an extent, on the auditor's mandate. For example, in Ireland, the C&AG is permitted to examine:

- whether and to what extent the resources of a body have been used economically and efficiently
- the systems, procedures and practices employed by a body in evaluating the effectiveness of its operations.

It should be noted that this is a relatively narrow mandate. The C&AG has a role in evaluating not the effectiveness of policies or even the effectiveness of operations, but rather the quality of the systems, procedures and practices used by the body itself to evaluate the effectiveness of its operations.

Examinations of this kind are usually referred to as VFM examinations. Normally, about ten to twelve VFM reports are produced each year and about 10 per cent of the resources of the office are devoted to it.

The contribution of performance audits to improved public sector performance is the subject of debate and experiment in several countries, as follows.

- The Comptroller General of the United States is supported by the Government Accountability Office (GAO). Unusually, the GAO puts little emphasis on financial auditing – almost all its work consists of programme evaluation. It has a staff of about 3,300 covering many professions and produces about 1,000 reports a year. It functions like a management consultancy and produces reports that tend to focus on recommendations aimed at improving accountability, operations and services. While this

approach has much to commend it, one should remember
that the legislative and constitutional context in which the
GAO operates is radically different to that in Ireland.

- In the United Kingdom, the performance audit mandate is
broader than in Ireland, covering economy, efficiency and
operational effectiveness. Output is about 60 reports per
annum, consuming about 25 per cent of the NAO's
resources. In New Zealand, the mandate is the same as in
the United Kingdom. Output is about 15 reports per
annum and uses about 15 per cent of audit resources.

- In Australia, officials indicated that the ANAO produces
about 50 performance audit reports per annum, representing only about one or two per portfolio per annum.
Nevertheless, it believes that these reports are an important feature of the accountability framework. The ANAO
has described its performance audit services as the
'primary' contributor to its sought outcome of improvement in public administration. However, it also sees performance audit reports as providing significant assurance
to parliament about how an area of public administration
is being conducted.

This view of performance audit as having a dual role is not
unique to the ANAO. The international auditing standard on
performance audits confirms that performance audit is a
flexible concept that, depending on the auditor's perspective,
can be used either as a tool for encouraging performance
improvement or as an accountability mechanism. (INTOSAI,
2004).

Conclusions on the role of national audit

Although some national audit offices, such as the NAO in the
UK and the GAO in the USA, publish data claiming to quan-
tify savings arising from improvements brought about as a
result of their performance audits, the precise contribution of
performance audit to improving the performance of public
sector organisations may prove difficult to measure.
However, it seems at least likely that it can play a useful role
as part of a broader focus on performance in reformed

accountability systems. Along with the identification of best practice, and the validation of performance reporting systems and data, it offers an opportunity – and a significant challenge – for national audit offices to play an important and positive role in helping to construct a performance culture in the public service and to reinforce the other elements of the trend towards accountability for performance and delivery discussed in this chapter.

Conclusions and recommendations

The role and principles of effective accountability

This chapter has considered accountability arrangements in the context of their impact on performance and delivery. It has noted a trend towards new or modified accountability systems in several countries. These developments are closely linked to the emergence of new organisational structures in the public service, but also impact heavily on the core Civil Service. The evolving accountability systems are playing an increasingly central part in determining the role of senior civil servants and their relationships with ministers and others.

Accountability systems are focused on three broad purposes:

- providing for democratic monitoring and control of public administration
- avoiding misuse of concentration of power and providing assurance of propriety
- encouraging improved performance through reporting on achievements and learning.

In Ireland, our existing systems have generally proved effective in the first two of these roles, although this is increasingly being questioned. However, there can be no doubt that our accountability systems have not been focused on performance improvement. They are more focused on process than on outcome and have some important negative side-effects, including acting as disincentives to innovation and risk-taking. Changes in legislation, and through the SMI, in recent years are beginning to address this, but we can and should do much more to ensure that our accountability systems underpin and encourage high performance.

In doing so, we would do well to observe the five principles for effective accountability identified by the Canadian Auditor General (2002):

- identify clear roles and responsibilities
- ensure clear performance expectations
- provide for the appropriate balance of expectations and capacities
- provide credible and timely reporting
- ensure fair and informed review and feedback on performance and appropriate consequences.

Accountability and the budget/report/audit cycle

Accountability, to be meaningful, must be considered with reference to the resources available to achieve performance. Budgeting and accounting practice are, therefore, key aspects of the accountability framework.

In many countries, this is linked with accountability for 'non-financial' performance. 'Performance management' is an ever-stronger mantra. This is reflected in our work in Ireland on strategy statements and annual reports at organisation level, and PMDS at individual level.

There is a desire to understand what has been spent and what has been achieved with this spending. This is required at both the level of the individual organisation and the aggregate level of total public spending. It is a strong and increasing demand from the political system, although in Ireland it has not been matched by an engagement on the part of politicians with the performance measurement systems that have been put in place through SMI.

This is the thinking that underlies the effort on management information framework (MIF) in recent years, and more recently the new AOS/estimates process. It also underpins the more developed PB systems in Australia, New Zealand, the UK and elsewhere, which seek to measure resources used, outputs delivered and outcomes achieved in a more ambitious way than in our current systems.

Performance budgeting

An alternative to our existing systems is, therefore, possible. It would begin with a clear statement of what is to be achieved, linked to the organisation's annual budget, and would then report performance on both financial and non-financial targets. This is the approach encapsulated in the PB systems in the NPM countries.

It is important to note that PB is not a new idea and some previous experience in Ireland and abroad has not been very positive. Nevertheless, it is now a very strong trend internationally. It is, as Schick (2003) points out, 'an old idea, whose time has come'.

In Ireland, we are heading cautiously towards PB. With the implementation of modern accounts systems in recent years and the work on performance management through the SMI, PMDS and MIF processes we have, in principle, already put in place some of the basic building blocks for PB.

Process and behaviour: the role of ministers and civil servants

A key point, made by the OECD and others, is that an effective PB system requires not only new processes, but also changed behaviour by politicians, the Department of Finance and management in line departments. The experience in the countries we have examined indicates that PB must be implemented within a broader framework of devolved control of resources, and a strong focus on results in political debate and administrative oversight systems. The AOS initiative in 2007 and 2008 will provide an important test of whether this is likely to occur in Ireland.

Arguably, however, this experiment comes at a somewhat awkward time. Clarification of the role of secretaries general/ accounting officers in recent years, and in particular the introduction of the 1997 PSM Act, has been positive but has not been sufficient to deal with the need to define fully the relationships between ministers, secretaries general and other officials in a way that seems appropriate to the twenty-first century. The Carltona doctrine remains in place but is increasingly questioned by leading figures, including those directly affected by it. An open and well-informed debate is required to create the rounded understanding of the issues that is a necessary first step to resolving them. However, there is currently no space in which to have this debate between all the key participants. It is essential that this gap be filled, as there is a need to undertake a fundamental review of the relationship between ministers and officials and to define clear and balanced rights, responsibilities and accountability relationships. The Institute of Public Administration, or another academic institution, might facilitate such a debate. It might also be addressed in the review of the Irish public administration being conducted by the OECD for the Department of the Taoiseach. It has been suggested that it will look at 'the quality and clarity of the linkages and channels between ministers and their departments and other agencies under their aegis'.

Clarity on this fundamental issue is also necessary if we are to determine what contribution PB might make to effective accountability, and what changes in behaviour by ministers, the political opposition, the C&AG and PAC, the Department of Finance and departmental management is required to achieve this. It must therefore be stressed that a move to PB cannot be seen as simply a technical decision to change budget processes.

Accrual budgeting and reporting

An important technical issue that will arise is whether it is desirable or necessary to move to accrual budgeting and reporting as part of the development of PB. Much work has been done on the use of accrual accounts in the public service and there are now significant examples of this, both in accrual budgeting in the NPM countries and in the production of accruals reports by non-commercial state agencies in Ireland. This evidence, however, does not allow an unambiguous conclusion that the significant effort required to move to accruals would be worthwhile. Accrual accounting can facilitate good financial management and, in particular, can clarify the real cost of projects and programmes. It also avoids some perverse incentives of cash accounting. But the superior information provided by accruals is of little value unless budget holders have real discretion on how budgets are spent, and have the financial knowledge and skills necessary to use accruals information effectively to support their decision-making. Neither of these conditions is currently satisfied in the Irish Civil Service.

The following recommendations are therefore made.

- We should embark on a process of recruitment and internal skills development to put in place a significantly enhanced level of accounting expertise. This will facilitate a subsequent move to accruals but is, in any case, necessary in the short term to obtain full value from the modern accounts systems now being installed.
- We should provide for a greater degree of devolved control within the terms of our current administrative and programme budget systems. Without devolved financial controls there would be little point in moving to accruals.

With these arrangements in place we should adopt accrual budgeting and reporting, as part of a decisive move to PB, once the response to the new AOS has been assessed. If that assessment leads to a decision to adopt a fully-fledged PB framework, with devolved authority and accountability, then the effort and cost involved in a move to accruals would be justified. It is critical that such a decision have strong political backing.

Reporting on non-financial performance

Non-financial performance reporting is the other key element of the new accountability processes. As noted above, we have in recent years – and in conformity with international practice – put in place fairly elaborate, formal performance reporting systems through strategy statements and annual reports, the PMDS and the MIF. However, performance measurement and management systems are very uneven in the Irish Civil Service and are not, in practice, well developed in many departments.

If the AOS system is to represent a significant step towards a more performance-oriented accountability system it is vital that the information contained in the AOS is concise, meaningful, and genuinely useful for understanding what is achieved with public funds. The Taoiseach's decision to ask the Implementation Group of Secretaries General to review this information is, therefore, very welcome. It is recommended that this should grow into a formal system of regular external validation of the performance indicators (PIs) used in the AOS, perhaps by the C&AG. These PIs should be reflected in departments' strategy statements and annual reports, and this validation process would enhance the useful content of these documents.

A new role for national audit

Validation of performance information may well become a key role for the C&AG in a future performance-focused accountability system.

The focus of the work of national audit offices in other countries examined in this dissertation is also increasingly shifting to performance auditing, augmenting the attest work of such offices. In Ireland, the C&AG currently devotes a modest 10 per cent of staff time to VFM reports. It is recommended that this be expanded and that particular attention be given to identifying examples of best practice that can be emulated. This type of work is the main focus of national audit in some other countries, including the USA. The current almost exclusive focus of C&AG reports, and PAC hearings, on deficiencies found in the course of the annual audit acts as a strong incentive to avoid breaches of correct procedure, but does little to encourage high performance. It would therefore be a poor match for a modern, performance-based budgeting and accountability system.

5

Leading for performance and delivery

In this chapter we look at how the Civil Service might go about acquiring and developing its future leaders. While we recognise that high-performing public service organisations will require leadership at all levels, our concern in this chapter is with leadership at senior management level.

The OECD (2001) has identified public service leadership as a critical component of good public governance and has suggested that the changing environment requires a new type of leadership. It defines the quest for more leadership in the public sector as the search for 'people who will promote institutional adaptations in the public interest'. It suggests that leadership, in this sense, is not value-neutral but rather a positive espousal of the need to promote certain fundamental values that can be called public-spiritedness.

A focus on leadership is important because the kinds of structural changes and changes to accountability that we argue for elsewhere in this volume are not guaranteed, of themselves, to bring about better performance. Indeed, there is a danger that without the right leadership, accountability for performance will become little more than a game designed to justify existing performance and protect the organisation from external criticism. For example, Ingraham (2001) cites the Government Performance Project – a large-scale review of performance in US state governments and federal agencies – as concluding that, without leadership commitment, managing-for-results systems became just another paper-generating activity.

Leadership also acquires an increased significance as the emphasis changes from a concern with managing inputs to managing for outcomes. The OECD (2001) has suggested that the role of leadership in this is to support the cultural change that a move to managing for outcomes entails, to motivate staff for this task, and to facilitate cooperation across departmental boundaries.

We begin with a brief exploration of what leadership means in the context of the public sector and why it has received considerable attention internationally in recent years. We consider the nature of the challenge that Ireland faces in this area.

In the course of the discussion we deal with three particular challenges in acquiring, developing and retaining the right leadership:

- recruitment and selection
- reward
- leadership development.

We then look at how senior management is selected or recruited. We explore the basic choice between, on one hand, recruiting people at an entry level and developing them to lead the organisation in the future and, on the other hand, recruiting senior management directly. Thereafter we look at the question of reward and consider the effectiveness of performance-related pay. Finally we deal with leadership development and consider the options for identifying and developing talent within the organisation.

Leadership in the public sector

What is leadership and why is it important?

Leadership can be defined as a 'social influence process' (OECD, 2001), a 'relationship through which one person influences the behaviour or actions of other people' (Mullins, 2002) or 'the process in which an individual influences other group members towards the attainment of group or organisational objectives' (Shackleton, 2005). Leadership is about motivation, interpersonal behaviour and communication; it is a two-way process between leader and followers (Mullins, 2002).

Table 5.1: Competency model for secretary general and assistant secretary positions

Generic competency domains	Leadership	Judgement relationships	Managing	Personal drive for results
Secretary general	• Establishing vision and purpose • Providing developmental leadership	• Judgement and systemic perspective • Steering through the political environment • Environmental awareness	• Managing relationships • Communication	• Managing for results • Personal drive and accountability • Professional integrity
Assistant secretary	• Leads on the management of change • Focus on human resources • Corporate contribution	• Analysis and thinking skills • Strategic contribution	• Managing critical relationships • Communication	• Organisational skills • Results-oriented approach • Professional integrity

Source: Top Level Appointments Committee (TLAC) (2002)

According to the OECD (2001), interest in public service leadership has had a resurgence in many countries in recent years. This interest has centred on four ideas:

- the changing environment requires a new type of leadership
- the focus of leadership is changing
- leadership is different from management
- new leadership involves all levels of the organisation.

As regards changing environment, the argument is that new approaches to leadership are necessary that are better fitted for the tasks of redesigning, renovating or reinventing existing organisations, as well as securing coherence, accountability, and coordination between policies and various interests.

The focus of leadership is changing because, as a result of various social changes, including more mobility and job opportunity, today's public service leaders need to get *commitment* from their followers, not just *compliance*. They have to find ways beyond their authority to influence their followers effectively.

The terms 'management' and 'leadership' are frequently used with the same meaning, and there is certainly overlap between them. The difference is largely one of emphasis. Management relates more to formal systems, processes and incentives. Leadership is more about informal influence – how to mobilise people through values and visions.

Leadership is relevant at all levels of the organisation, and not only in respect of the higher positions within the hierarchy. Thus, for example, the US administration distinguishes three levels of leadership, namely strategic leadership, team leadership and technical leadership (OECD, 2001). Similarly, it has been suggested that the opinion leaders in most organisations are not the senior managers but the front-line supervisors, who play a crucial role in changing behaviour within organisations (Larkin and Larkin, 1996).

Our concern in this chapter is with leadership at senior levels in the organisation. In particular, we are addressing the issue of how the Civil Service can best acquire and develop the kind of senior leadership that will promote performance and delivery. This is in line with the approach in other countries that have introduced public sector reforms and where there has been a special emphasis on the senior Civil Service. The role of senior civil servants is considered to be critical to give a clear sense of direction to policy formulation, to improve performance, and to deliver services effectively. Leadership is regarded as critical to leading change, inspiring staff, increasing performance and strengthening values. However, as the OECD (2005a) has pointed out, improving performance and reinforcing collective service culture and values may, at times, become conflicting objectives.

The challenge for Ireland

We believe that the challenge for Ireland centres not on trying to decide what kind of leadership the Civil Service needs, but on the practical problem of how to acquire it. We say this because the leadership competencies identified for senior civil servants (see Table 5.1) seem to capture all the essential aspects of the kind of leadership identified as desirable in the OECD studies.

To set the challenge in context when making international comparisons, it is necessary to understand where Ireland sits in the spectrum of Civil Service models. Traditionally, there have been two basic models of Civil Service systems, namely 'career-based' systems and 'position-based' systems. In career-based systems public servants are expected to stay in the public service more or less throughout their working life. Promotion is based on a system of grades attached to the individual rather than to a specific position. Generally such a system affords limited possibilities for entering the Civil Service mid-career.

Position-based systems focus on selecting the best-suited candidate for each position, whether by external recruitment or internal promotion. Position-based systems tend to allow more open access, and lateral entry is relatively common. In position-based systems the senior Civil Service generally consists of top managers and an identified pool of potential top managers. In career-based systems the senior Civil Service consists of a broader echelon, which may range down to lower management levels. In general, the Irish Civil Service is very much to the career-based end of the spectrum although, as discussed below, this is changing somewhat. The change is in line with a trend identified by the OECD (2005a) for position-based systems to become more centralised as regards the management of senior managers, and career-based systems to become more open to external competition, with the result that the distinction between the two systems is less and less clear.

The question of whether a career-based or a position-based system is superior is controversial. For example, Turnbull

(2005) argues strongly in favour of having a majority of lifelong civil servants on the basis that the strength of the Civil Service as an organisation depends on its values. This view is challenged by Darwall (2005), who claims that it focuses on values rather than effectiveness.

We do not consider further the relative merits of the two systems. Instead, we consider how the practical problem of acquiring and developing leadership talent can be addressed given our existing system but adopting, where we consider it advisable, features of the alternative position-based system.

Recruitment and selection

Entry-level recruitment

As discussed above, the challenge involved in acquiring leadership talent differs between career-based and position-based systems. In the former, the challenge is to recruit the best available people at entry level, retain them and develop them to eventually become leaders. In the latter, the challenge is to recruit, from the market, people with an existing track record of leadership, in a way that does not have negative side-effects such as weakening the public service ethos.

Table 5.2: Civil Service external recruitment activity

Category of appointment	Number of appointment processes announced	Number of applications received	Number of appointments made
Professional	59	1,703	102
Technical	9	5,024	19
Managerial	24	498	13
General service	7	25,906	607
Departmental	7	5,053	226
Temporary clerical	1	8,411	45
Total	107	46,595	1,012

Source: 2005 Annual Report of the Commission for Public Service Appointments

In Ireland, open recruitment takes place at three entry levels – clerical officer, executive officer and administrative officer. On the surface, at any rate, the Civil Service does not seem to have much difficulty in attracting potential recruits. The ratio of applicants to number of appointments in 2005, as shown in Table 5.2, would seem to support this.

From the figures given in Table 5.2, it is not clear whether the Civil Service attracts sufficient top graduates. This is an area that would merit further research. We note that the Public Appointments Service has initiated a research advisory panel to examine issues in the areas of recruitment, selection, assessment and development that are of relevance to the public sector and HR practitioners in general. The panel has drawn up a research programme to help advance thinking and understanding in a number of areas including attracting top-quality people to the public service.

Previous research, however, would suggest that there is a potentially serious problem. O'Riordan and Humphreys (2002) quote two research studies conducted in 1999, the first among new recruits and the second among non-Civil Service employees and young people. New recruits were generally satisfied with their career choice but regarded the Civil Service as significantly inferior to foreign multinationals and major Irish companies in offering competitive salaries. Non-employees and young people generally regarded the Civil Service as inferior to the private sector in its capacity to:

- offer promotion based on ability and performance
- provide interesting and varied work and a happy working environment
- look after the welfare of its staff
- pay competitive salaries.

The research concluded that more able candidates are increasingly lured into the private sector either immediately on graduating or after a number of years in the service, and indicated the need to raise awareness of the Civil Service, to improve its image and to position it alongside other employers as a provider of rewarding and fulfilling careers.

O'Riordan and Humphreys (2002) also quote research by

Goldsmith Fitzgerald (1999) which found that the retention of staff at senior levels in the Irish Civil Service was not an issue. At assistant principal (AP) level and above, the staff turnover rate is minimal. O'Riordan & Humphreys suggest that one reason for this is that such positions, in general, are more varied and carry greater responsibility, and are therefore more satisfying. However, this may be a rather sanguine view. The Goldsmith Fitzgerald research suggested that at levels below AP there were three majors factors driving resignations: earnings and career progression; task responsibility; reward and recognition. According to Goldsmith Fitzgerald, there is a yawning gap between individuals' aspirations in respect of these factors and what the Civil Service is perceived as delivering.

Entry-level recruitment – the international experience

The challenge faced by Ireland in recruiting potential future leaders via the normal entry grades is not unique. We found that Australia and New Zealand had a number of incentives at various levels, designed to attract and retain potential future leaders.

In Australia the Graduate Recruitment Scheme (GRS) is a 12-month development programme, offering the opportunity to learn about government and contribute to a range of policy initiatives. Graduates recruited by a particular department commence on what is regarded as an attractive entry-level salary. They undertake up to three placements in different work areas and departments, and on satisfactory completion of the programme return to a permanent role in their original department at a higher grade. They are entitled to leave and other normal entitlements during this period. A part-time equivalent employment can also be arranged in most departments. The scheme is highly regarded in all areas of Australian government.

The Public Sector Cadetship Programme targets people who are disadvantaged in the labour market. Cadets combine formal training at certificate, diploma or advanced diploma levels with paid work experience in a public sector agency.

New Zealand also offers a cadetship programme for school leavers to provide young people with a career path in the public sector and quality training linked to a modern apprenticeship scheme and working towards industry qualifications. The aim of the programme is to reinforce the capacity of the public sector by recruiting, developing and retaining young people with the ability to become future leaders. The cadets are full-time employees and undertake study over a two-year period to obtain a certificate in customer service in the public sector.

Conclusions

In our view it is hard to avoid the conclusion that even where the Civil Service succeeds in attracting young, able and ambitious people at entry level, it faces a significant challenge in retaining them at least up to assistant principal level. Clearly, this has serious consequences for any leadership acquisition strategy that relies exclusively on the traditional approach of recruiting people at entry level and developing them within the service so that they will eventually take on leadership positions.

A revitalisation of the administrative officer recruitment scheme is one practical step that could be taken to improve the attractiveness of the Civil Service to top graduates. While some departments appear to use the scheme as it was originally envisaged, practice is not uniform throughout the Civil Service.

The scheme should be specifically marketed as a top-level graduate recruitment scheme, with a clear and specific commitment to training and development through mobility and with guaranteed promotion, subject to satisfactory service, within five years.

Recruitment at the middle grades

Ireland

One recent change that has implications for the traditional strategy of recruiting potential leaders at entry level and developing them within the service is the opening up of some positions at assistant principal and above to external recruitment. *Towards 2016* provides that the Civil Service may recruit by open competition in any year:

- two in nine of all vacancies at principal officer (standard and higher scales) and equivalent grades, including equivalent professional and technical grades
- one in five of all vacancies at assistant principal officer (standard and higher scales) and equivalent grades, including equivalent professional and technical grades
- one in six of all vacancies at higher executive officer and equivalent grades, including equivalent professional and technical grades.

Most of the recruitments to fulfil the above quotas will be made through generic competitions for appointment to general service posts. However, some of this recruitment may be used to meet specialised requirements in general service posts and will be part of the quotas shown above.

Recruitment at assistant principal and above has to be seen as at least an implicit acknowledgement that the traditional strategy of relying on entry-level recruitment is no longer effective. It also implies that Ireland's system is envisaged as remaining towards the career-based end of the spectrum of Civil Service systems. Thus, it is envisaged that recruits at this level will have the same terms and conditions of service as other civil servants, including tenure. Crucially, the restriction of the proportion of posts that can be filled by open competition is a recognition that the implied contract with entry-level recruits – that they will be offered development opportunities and access to the highest posts – is to remain in place.

International experience

Open recruitment at middle levels of the Civil Service may be seen as part of the trend identified by the OECD of career-based and position-based systems becoming more like one another. However, we were unable to gather any evidence from our study trip to Australia and New Zealand of how successful the strategy outlined in *Towards 2016* is likely to be. This is because the systems in both these countries have moved very far from the traditional career-based model.

In Australia, for example, the approach to staffing the public service (APS) is the same as that applying in the workforce generally. The public service therefore operates as far as possible, consistent with its public responsibilities, under the same industrial relations and employment arrangements as apply generally.

Agency heads have direct power over engagement of staff, as well as authority to determine their remuneration and terms and conditions of employment, although this power must be exercised within parameters set by the government. Almost all recruitment to the public service is by open competition. Around 45 per cent of all employees recruited during 2001–2 were working in the private sector prior to entering the APS.

Recruitment and selection of senior civil servants

The choice between the traditional route and hiring-in of leaders

The limitations of recruiting future leaders from the original entry-level pool are now well understood. Ingraham (2001) summarises them as:

- a difficulty in transforming the narrow perspective acquired over time by such entrants, who may remain for long periods in a particular 'stove-pipe' of expertise or experience, into a broader institutional view
- a possible lack of diversity at the levels of the organisation that create the feeder pool for leaders, and a consequent continuing lack of diversity in the leadership cadre.

An increase in cross-departmental promotion competitions – in place for some years and due to expand under *Towards 2016* – as well as the proposal to recruit at the middle levels can be understood as responses to these perceived limitations.

The solution proposed by the NPM reforms to the limitations of the traditional route is quite different, namely to 'buy' or hire in leadership talent and to explicitly adopt private sector contract models for the senior Civil Service. However, as Ingraham (2001) points out, this approach has the following limitations.

- Those hired in this way may have limited capabilities in understanding and committing to core public service values.
- Blending of internal and external talents and perspectives in a leadership cadre requires careful balancing if it is not to lead to a fractured and fractious leadership group.

Ingraham (2001) also suggests that a new approach to hiring leaders cannot, of itself, improve public sector performance and that there are certain preconditions for performance, not least the extent to which leaders and managers have the necessary tools, skills, and organisational capability to attain performance objectives.

Ireland's experience

In Ireland, a new model for the selection of assistant secretaries and higher grades was adopted in 1984 when the Top Level Appointments Committee (TLAC) was established. Its aim was to ensure that only candidates who merited such promotions were successful (TLAC, 1998a).

The competencies considered initially in these appointments appeared to be weighted in favour of technical expertise or specialism. In 1998, TLAC signalled that this would change and that henceforth more emphasis would be placed on the candidate's ability in driving the modernising change agenda (TLAC, 1998b).

TLAC has the discretion to decide that posts coming within its remit should be filled by open competition. However, it did so in only eight out of a total of 223 instances between 1984 and 1997 (TLAC, 1998a).

There is no doubt that the establishment of TLAC has increased mobility in the higher levels of the Civil Service. Of 223 competitions, apart from secretary general level, 177 were at assistant secretary level; 136 of these were to the general service grades and 41 to professional grades, and 54 (32 per cent) involved movement from one department to another. However, an analysis of the statistics (see Table 5.3) suggests that in recent years there has been a sharp decline in the success rates of candidates from outside the appointing department, from 28 per cent in 1995–9 to 15 per cent in 2000–4.

Table 5.3: Success rates of internal and external candidates

Year	No. of applicants	Internal successes	External successes
1995	459	13	6
1996	124	4	2
1997	481	16	5
1998	232	10	5
1999	123	8	2
2000	305	18	4
2001	217	11	4
2002	249	19	2
2003	111	6	1
2004	107	10	0

Source: Tuohy, 2005

The statistics given in Table 5.3 might suggest that knowledge specific to the post on offer is a significant factor in appointments, contrary to TLAC's assertion that more emphasis would be placed on the candidate's ability in driving the modernising change agenda. Certainly, the identified competencies for senior Civil Service posts (see above) do emphasise competencies associated with change management. However, if the published competencies are the sole criteria used in selection then the outcome noted above is a surprising one.

Of course, the outcome may be influenced significantly by the perceptions of prospective candidates. It is noteworthy that the average number of applicants per advertised post fell sharply from twenty in 1995–9 to thirteen in 2000–4. So, it may be that potentially suitable candidates outside a department are discouraged by their perception that internal candidates have significant advantages – something that ought not to be the case in a true competency-based system.

Whatever the reason, it is clear that the TLAC system's influence as a force that promotes mobility between departments on promotion to assistant secretary has declined significantly. In addition, there is no mechanism to permit interdepartmental mobility at assistant secretary level, nor is there any service-wide policy on mobility at that level within departments.

The Taoiseach (2006) seemed to recognise this lack of mobility as a weakness when he invited the SMI Implementation Group of Secretaries General to develop a new leadership initiative for the public service. He emphasised some of the practical steps that he saw as necessary:

- organising career development and succession planning
- providing the right mix of specialist staff, who have developed careers through areas such as human resources, finance or project management
- ensuring that people in senior positions have had a sufficient breadth of experience, across departments and agencies and also across different types of management responsibility
- developing and supporting those in key areas of responsibility and leadership so as to encourage greater cooperation and mobility across the branches of the public service.

International experience

The approach to the recruitment of senior civil servants in Australia and New Zealand is very different. In New Zealand, the public service (subject to the State Services Act) is made up of 35 departments and other state services including crown entities and crown agents, and employs about 190,000 people. Each agency has a chief executive as its administrative head, with duties modelled on the private sector equivalent.

Chief executives are recruited through the State Services Commission both internally and externally. Contract periods are usually for five years. Chief executive performance is subject to political scrutiny, of course, but also to scrutiny from the State Services Commission, a department whose mandate is to ensure that each agency within its remit reaches its 'development goals' as set out in its statement of intent.

Chief executive performance is reviewed in the context of the 'Management for Outcomes Programme' (a model of management that measures outcomes rather than outputs). Failure to achieve these organisational goals will militate against reappointment of a chief executive (State Services Commission, 2005).

In Australia, the Senior Executive Service (SES), the leadership cadre of the Australian public service (APS), was created in 1984 with the aim of making the service at senior levels more open, mobile and competitive and to achieve a greater degree of management leadership in the development and the placement of senior staff. The intention was to reshape the cadre of senior employees into a more unified and cohesive group responsible for higher-level policy advice, managerial and professional responsibilities. All SES vacancies are open to applicants from outside the service as well as to serving officials. Arrangements for staff selection, development, mobility, promotion and tenure are designed specifically to meet common requirements at senior levels. Recruitment to the SES from outside the APS has fluctuated substantially over the years – ranging from 14 per cent in 2000–1 to 25 per cent in 1992–3 – with no trend becoming apparent.

Secretaries of departments are engaged on five-year contracts and, in practice, contracts are usually renewed. While there has been some increase in mobility in and out of the

APS at secretary level, the vast majority of secretaries are career public servants with a proven record of performance.

Discussions with New Zealand and Australian HR practitioners during our study trip tended to confirm some of the difficulties with the hiring-in solution identified by Ingraham (2001). Typical of the views expressed were comments that the system had led to too much 'churning'. This tended to lead to a loss in long-term planning/thinking. One official suggested that his organisation was in danger of totally losing corporate knowledge. Another described the system as 'ending up with attempts to retrofit more collectivity onto the highly individualised system that you get in the individual contract system' and suggested that what was really needed was for the public service to learn to work better with the people it has got.

Reward mechanisms

The concept of reward in the public sector

As Boyle (1997b) has pointed out, creating appropriate reward mechanisms for good performance in the Civil Service is a challenging task. There is not the same freedom as in the private sector to introduce bonuses or offer 'perks' such as company cars and holidays. The definition of what constitutes outstanding performance can be difficult. Boyle suggests that to be effective, reward mechanisms need to be adapted to the requirements of the workforce, and to combine a mix of 'extrinsic' (salary and benefits) and 'intrinsic' (feelings of competence, achievement, responsibility, challenge, accomplishment and independence) rewards.

Based on a brief review of international research, Boyle tentatively concluded that public servants tend to value intrinsic over extrinsic rewards. Public and private sector managers valued intrinsic rewards equally, but private sector managers placed a higher value on extrinsic rewards.

On the other hand, if hiring-in from the private sector were a significant element of the strategy for acquiring new leadership talent, it would be naive to believe that level of extrinsic reward would not be a key factor for many able people in deciding whether to move. We now consider this issue with reference to base salaries and performance-related pay.

Base salaries

The remuneration of senior civil servants is set by the government after considering the recommendations of the Review Body on Higher Remuneration in the Public Sector, a standing body established in 1969 to advise the government from time to time. In making its recommendations the Review Body has regard to the level of remuneration in jobs that are considered comparable in the private sector. The last full review conducted by the Review Body, in 2000, recommended that basic pay for the top posts in the public service should be benchmarked to the lower quartile of the private sector, as a medium-term objective. As a first step, it was recommended that most salaries should be brought up to around 85 per cent of the lowest quartile. For a small number of non-commercial state companies where private sector rates are more relevant, a 95 per cent salary level was considered to be more appropriate.

The Review Body conducted an interim review in 2005, which recommended an interim award but declined to recommend an increase that would bring the salaries of senior public servants beyond 85 per cent of the lowest quartile. Another full review is to be completed in 2007. In the 2005 interim review it indicated that one issue that it would examine in 2007 is the value of public sector pension arrangements. It suggested that the value of public service pensions is a critical factor in any comparison with rates of remuneration in the private sector. It said that it intended to consider the extent to which the value of public service superannuation arrangements should be offset against the remuneration packages available in the private sector.

What is clear from the foregoing is that there is no prospect of salary levels for senior civil servants being set above the lowest quartile of comparable private sector employment – if they even reach this level. In the circumstances, if leadership talent is to be hired in from the private sector then the remuneration packages on offer may well have to be different from those available to existing civil servants. In effect, it seems possible that individualised contracts will be necessary to attract the necessary talent.

It is worth noting that individualised contracts involving levels of remuneration well in excess of other public sector jobs are not unknown in the non-commercial semi-state sector. However, within the Civil Service this is likely to prove problematic in the light of evidence gathered during our study trip to Australia and New Zealand.

During our meetings with agencies in these countries, three particular problems with individualised contracts were identified. First, there was a perception that the system was becoming extremely cumbersome and difficult to handle, even though the actual number of individual contracts was still comparatively small. Second, in Australia, we were informed that when staff change agencies at the same grade they are allowed to maintain their existing salary level if this is higher than the salary that the new employer might otherwise offer. This has led to some big disparities in pay between staff at the same level within an agency, which can be a serious source of resentment. Third, individualised contracts have led to competition between agencies for staff.

Performance-related pay

OECD (2005a) research has concluded that the impact of performance related pay (PRP) on motivation is varied: while it appears to motivate a minority of staff, it seems that a large majority do not see PRP as an incentive. While base pay according to the wider 'market' is important, supplementary pay increases for performance are a second-rank incentive for government employees, especially those in non-managerial roles. Job content and career development perspectives have been found to be the strongest incentives for public employees. PRP is unlikely to motivate a substantial majority irrespective of design.

On a more positive note, the OECD (2005a) concluded that PRP facilitates other organisational changes. These include an improved and stronger focus on effective appraisal and goal-setting processes as well as clarification of tasks, better attention to the acquisition of skills and teamwork, the improvement of employee–manager dialogue, and increased flexibility in work organisation. According to the OECD, PRP can facilitate a renegotiation of the 'effort bargain', thus assisting in recasting the culture at the workplace.

The OECD conclusions relate to PRP for the workforce as a whole, but the question arises as to whether the same argument holds true for the leadership cadre. After all, shouldn't a focus on effective appraisal and goal-setting processes and increased flexibility be expected from the organisation's leaders, regardless of whether pay is linked to performance?

Notwithstanding this doubt, we believe that PRP is part of the landscape and is likely to remain so. The Review Body (2005) has found that for senior posts in the private sector the proportion of remuneration linked to performance is rising. So, it may be expected that PRP will form a fairly significant element of contracts offered to private sector managers to induce them to join the public sector. In the circumstances it is worth looking at the Irish experience of PRP to see whether there are any changes that might be needed if it is to deliver the benefits that the OECD suggests are possible.

PRP – the Irish experience

The current system of performance awards for assistant secretaries and chief executives of state bodies was introduced in 2001 on foot of recommendations from the Review Body. Under the scheme, the pool for performance awards for assistant secretaries is 10 per cent of the pay bill for the group concerned. Within that overall limit, individuals can receive payments of up to 20 per cent of pay.

A previous scheme was heavily criticised by the Review Body, which felt that it had not been operated as originally intended. It pointed out that, in the case of the non-commercial state-sponsored bodies, the chief executive was in almost every case awarded the maximum possible bonus in each year. It said that it is fundamentally wrong to regard performance-related awards as a way of supplementing what some might regard as inadequate basic pay.

The Review Body also criticised the operation of the scheme in the Civil Service, pointing out that most assistant secretaries were given an equal award. Some secretaries general indicated to the Review Body that they (i) placed greater emphasis on the development of a team ethic (than on individual excellence) and/or (ii) did not consider the resources available as sufficient to provide an incentive for better performance – views that the Review Body rejected. The arguments made about scarcity of resources were described as deriving from a culture that considers it neces-sary to ensure that some payment is made to everybody.

The Committee for Performance Awards oversees the current system. Similar concerns are expressed in its latest annual report (2005), although in much less trenchant terms. For example, the Committee pointed out that 76 per cent of awards were in the range 8 to 13 per cent, which it considered too narrow. It called for greater efforts to be made by heads of organisations to differentiate awards so that a high standard of performance is properly recognised and encouraged.

The experience of the performance award scheme is not dissimilar to the experience of how the exceptional merit award scheme has operated. This latter scheme is an initia-tive whereby departments can allocate 0.2 per cent of their administrative budget to pay in respect of exceptional performance. Departments have adopted varying approaches to the distribution of merit money, with some using it for social activities that all staff benefit from, which they claim are popular with staff. Others have stuck to the originally envisaged purpose of using it to reward individuals and groups for exceptional performance. Where exceptional merit awards money has been used in this way, allocating it to teams appears to be more favourably regarded by staff.

All in all it can be concluded that there is still a reluctance to assess performance in a frank way and to differentiate between individuals. In our view this is a problem that goes beyond PRP and raises questions about performance assessment generally.

PRP in Australia and New Zealand

In Australia all public service agencies link remuneration to individual performance in one way or another. The two most common approaches to performance-based remuneration are:

- *performance-linked advancement* – a base salary increase for satisfactory or higher performance, usually in terms of incremental progression either through pay points or through a percentage increase
- *performance-linked bonus* – usually a one-off bonus payment in recognition of higher than satisfactory performance.

Most remuneration schemes now link salary, rewards or bonuses, skill development and the work environment in their agency agreements. Agencies may give non-monetary rewards to individual employees in recognition of high achievement, such as formal awards, certificates or plaques, gift certificates, development opportunities, or conference attendance. Some agencies have adopted team-based reward systems, although not all have been successful.

In New Zealand, PRP systems are well defined for chief executives. On appointment of a new chief executive, the State Services Commissioner negotiates remuneration, and other terms and conditions, with the appointee. Performance incentives usually represent up to 15 per cent of the remuneration package. In addition, most agencies apply remuneration systems that include some form of lump sum performance payments for high performance over and above usual tasks. These are calculated as a percentage of base salary.

In Australia, surveys of the staff showed considerable scepticism as regards the impact of the system on actual performance. Many employees believed that the distribution of performance pay in their agency was unfair in that bias and favouritism were shown in performance reward decisions.

The situation in New Zealand is not very different. A survey of the public sector in 2005 also revealed a high level of staff dissatisfaction with the extent to which they perceived they had equitable access to rewards. There was a perception of inequities in the allocation of performance payments or bonuses.

Some scepticism was also noted in our discussions with officials in both Australia and New Zealand. The systems were perceived as very limited in financial terms in comparison with the ones applied in the private sector, and their effectiveness in terms of improving performance was regarded as negligible.

Some care is needed in interpreting these comments. Employee surveys in the APS have also highlighted dissatisfaction with performance appraisal, with the quality of the feedback given and with failures to deal with underperformance. It is also the case that levels of satisfaction with PRP vary across agencies (APS Commission, 2005) – something that led the Commission to conclude that some agencies had managed to establish more credible PRP systems than others. This could suggest that some, at least, of the dissatisfaction with PRP has its roots in dissatisfaction with the performance management system.

Conclusions

Despite the doubts about the effectiveness of PRP, it seems that it will remain a feature of the system in Ireland for senior civil servants. The comments of the Committee for Performance Awards suggest that it sees a reluctance on the part of secretaries general to differentiate between their reporting assistant secretaries, and that it does not believe that the system operates as it should.

It would be useful to gather the views of the assistant secretaries on the operation of the scheme; we recommend that this research be undertaken before any further changes to the scheme are made.

There is also the question of whether PRP in some shape or form ought to be extended to the Civil Service as a whole. Logically, if PRP is an important instrument in motivating and rewarding senior civil servants, why would it not be just as effective when applied to the service as a whole? Is it not one of the tools leaders and managers ought to have available to help build organisational capability to attain performance objectives?

Having reviewed the operation of PRP systems in Australia and New Zealand, we conclude that such a system has merit but that before it can be introduced the current PMDS system needs to function properly. From 2007 onwards PMDS faces a new challenge when appraisals begin to form the basis for increments and promotions. Only when we can be certain that PMDS does indeed meet this challenge will it be worth considering any extension of PRP to the rest of the Civil Service.

Leadership development

Why a leadership development strategy is needed

By a leadership development strategy we mean a strategy that identifies the particular kind of leadership that is desired in the future and then establishes programmes designed to make that kind of leadership available to the organisation. In a strict career-based system a strategy of that kind may be seen as unnecessary. In such a system, career progression – to the extent that it is not influenced by seniority – tends to depend on how the individual is perceived by the hierarchy, without individual members of the hierarchy necessarily having a shared view of why people should be promoted, let alone agreeing that leadership skills ought to be a significant factor.

One result of this could easily be that the leadership skills of each generation differ relatively little from those of the preceding one. This is not necessarily a problem provided that the environment changes relatively slowly. However, there is now a belief in some OECD countries, at least, that the environment has changed so much that new approaches to leadership, which are better fitted for the tasks of redesigning, renovating or reinventing existing organisations, are necessary. Following on from this, it is logical to try to define what the new leadership might look like and put in place a strategy to acquire it.

On a practical level there are also reasons why a clear leadership strategy, which can be publicly articulated, is vital. The first relates to the problem of attracting suitable leadership potential at the basic entry grade. Clearly, if the Civil Service cannot point to a strategy designed to develop talent and to offer attractive career progression, then the chances of attracting the right people are greatly reduced.

A similar argument holds for people joining at the middle grades. Indeed, the lack of a clear leadership strategy also has consequences for staff in the middle grades that have progressed from the basic entry grades. Under the current system, being in the right place at the right time or being lucky enough to have served in a department or section where staff development is given significant attention can influence how a person progresses. Such a system runs the risk that potential leadership talent is left unexploited, with a loss to both the individual and the organisation.

There is a further reason why a clear leadership development strategy is needed, i.e. the need to ensure that if people are recruited into the Civil Service at senior levels then the arrangements at the top are conducive to ensuring that – in Ingraham's (2001) words – the internal and external talent and perspectives are blended. We would have some concerns that the current system, where mobility of senior civil servants between departments is so low, would not be able to cope with the challenge of successfully inducting external recruits.

The international trend

Despite the apparently widespread concern in OECD countries with issues of public sector leadership, it is hard to detect a clear trend in terms of practical steps taken to develop future leaders. The OECD (2001) has identified three fairly general trends:

- the development of a comprehensive strategy for leadership selection and development
- setting up new institutions for leadership development
- linking existing training to leadership development.

In addition, there is a concern across countries about how to manage the senior Civil Service. This has given rise in a number of countries to the idea of what is usually referred to as a Senior Executive Service (SES) – a cadre of top civil servants managed separately to the rest of the service and with varying degrees of central intervention. It is clear that while the idea of an SES is fairly common, the practical arrangements differ greatly between countries and have tended to evolve to meet particular needs.

Leadership development in the Australian federal public service

In Australia, the Public Service Commissioner reviews employment policies and practices, coordinates training and has a specific mandate to contribute to and foster leadership. In line with this last responsibility, and to support its quality assurance role for SES appointments, the APS Commission has developed a framework identifying critical success factors for performance in APS leadership roles now and into the future. The leadership capabilities that make up the framework are that the individual:

- shapes strategic thinking
- achieves results
- cultivates productive working relationships
- exemplifies personal drive and integrity
- communicates with influence.

The APS Commission requires assessment against the five capabilities for all recruitment into the SES. The Commission also uses them for assessing development needs, including through 360-degree feedback (an evaluation process involving co-workers aimed at identifying all aspects of an employee's performance).

A Career Development Assessment Centre has been established to assess members of the SES feeder group to help identify their development needs for possible future promotion to the SES. It uses the Senior Executive Leadership Capability Framework in assessing participant performance through a series of formal scenario activities, and in supporting 360-degree feedback. Programme participants are provided with detailed feedback to guide their future development. The Assessment Centre has become an important part of succession planning in the APS, which has been promoted by the APS Commission since 1999–2000.

Management and leadership development initiatives are organised by both individual agencies and the APS Commission. Agencies typically contract external providers to deliver programmes specifically linked to their particular business, while the Commission's development programmes tend to focus on developing common leadership capabilities that support the strategic focus of the service.

The core programmes offered by the Commission include an orientation programme aimed at all new SES appointees, and a Senior Executive Leadership Programme involving more substantial and intensive development for those with a few years' SES experience. Other programmes include SES breakfasts, SES updates and lunchtime seminars. These are supplemented by *SES News*, a regular newsletter compiled by the APS Commission.

A further initiative is the Australia and New Zealand School of Government, which commenced operating in May 2003. It was established by a consortium of the Australian, Victorian, New South Wales, Queensland and New Zealand governments, and various universities. Its aim is to develop a future generation of public sector leaders by equipping them with the policy and management skills for an increasingly complex public service environment. It offers two core programmes, a two-year Master of Public Administration programme aimed at high-flying employees in the SES feeder group, and a short, intensive Fellowship programme aimed at top, experienced SES officers expected to be candidates for agency head positions.

As will be apparent from the foregoing description, the emphasis on leadership development in the Australian federal system is very much on formal programmes as well as the identification and development of staff in the 'feeder' groups. There is little emphasis on particular mechanisms to improve mobility. However, the reason for this is obvious – the system is so open that mobility is simply not a problem.

Leadership development in the New Zealand public service

One weakness in New Zealand's public management system identified by the *Review of the Centre* (2001) was shortcomings in the development of leaders and in the recruitment and training of staff with the right knowledge and skills.

Since then a new Executive Leadership Programme has been established to grow the talent pool at the top levels of the public sector. As many as 40 senior managers are inducted into the programme each year. The standard against which potential leaders are assessed is contained in the 'leadership capability profile'. This sets out the blueprint for New Zealand public service leaders, who:

- must have the required *personal attributes*
- which through a depth and breath of *experiences and pathways*
- will develop and deploy *leadership abilities*
- to deliver *results* for New Zealanders.

Candidates who are judged to meet the profile join the Executive Leadership Programme, through which the Leadership Development Centre delivers an individually tailored development programme. This programme has short, medium and long-term development components lasting over five years in order to develop specialist, leadership and management skills over time.

The programme has a target group of chief executives and tier 2 (second level) managers generally but may, depending on the size of the organisation, target tier 3 and 4 managers.

The programme includes in its academic component the

ANZSoG Executive Master of Administration Degree and the Executive Fellows programme. This sharing of the academic content of the programme with Australia requires mobility by the candidates between jurisdictions, giving participants the breadth of experience required of leaders.

In New Zealand, discussions with the State Services Commission suggested that they had difficulties in identifying the right people, but an even greater problem in getting people released for development. Chief executives tended to concentrate on their own deliverables and were not keen to be involved. However, the Commission believed that this problem is being overcome and that the scheme will gain more widespread acceptance.

As in Australia, the emphasis on leadership development in New Zealand is very much on formal programmes. Once again there is little emphasis on particular mechanisms to improve mobility, for the same reason as in Australia – the system is so open that mobility is not a problem.

The Irish experience

In Ireland, there is no central mechanism for identifying and developing potential leaders. The Taoiseach's comments on leadership are only the latest expression of unease at how the current system is operating. In 2002, a subgroup of the SMI Implementation Group of Secretaries General reported on this issue and recommended the establishment of a Senior Executive Service. It commented on the lack of interdepartmental mobility at assistant secretary level and suggested that this was one issue that the existence of an SES could address.

Another feature of the SES that the subgroup found would be of value in an Irish context was a systematic approach to developing senior civil servants through:

- challenging assignments
- interdepartmental mobility
- more robust selection procedures
- development programmes and mentoring
- establishment of 'candidate groups'

- external placement
- overseas assignments.

The report echoes many of the features of the Australian system, in particular, with a strong emphasis on establishing candidate groups along the lines of the feeder groups in Australia.

The report was noted by the government and circulated to the Civil Service unions for comment. No further action appears to have been taken other than to permit the extension of a secretary general's term from seven to ten years – representing a partial implementation of one of the group's proposals, made in the context of permitting greater mobility of secretaries general between departments. It is not clear to us why the group's recommendations have not proceeded further.

Conclusions and recommendations

The need to acquire the right kind of public service leadership for the future is a concern that Ireland shares with Australia and New Zealand, but the nature of the challenge is very different. In the latter countries, entry into the public service above the basic entry level is considered normal, and entrants at this level can have acquired a variety of experience. The challenge is largely one of blending internal and external talent and maintaining values.

According to Jack Welch, former CEO of General Electric, time spent on selecting the right person for the right job at the right time will have enormous strategic implications. We believe that under our current system not enough time and effort is put into leadership development and selection.

Appropriate structures, and performance-focused accountability systems, are vital components for an adaptive, effective and high-performance Civil Service in the twenty-first century. However, a senior leadership that is capable of using these structures and processes as a springboard to promote performance and delivery seems to us a vital third element.

In common with other countries, we currently face significant challenges in recruiting and retaining future leaders through the normal entry grades. Learning from experience in Australia and elsewhere, a revitalisation of the administrative officer recruitment scheme is necessary to improve the attractiveness of the Civil Service to top graduates. We recommend that the scheme be specifically marketed as a top graduate recruitment scheme, with a clear and specific commitment to training and to development through mobility, and with guaranteed promotion, subject to satisfactory service, within five years.

In Ireland, perhaps the key issue, identified by the Taoiseach (2006), is how to ensure that people in senior positions have had a sufficient breadth of experience, across departments and agencies and also across different types of management responsibility. In our view the opening up of middle-level and senior positions to more competition and to outside applicants will help, but will not necessarily guarantee the kind of leadership the Civil Service needs in the future.

We conclude that the current system militates against assistant secretaries acquiring the breadth of experience that the Taoiseach referred to. We recommend that the practice of the appointing department/office nominating internal candidates for the TLAC interview should cease, with a view to encouraging more interdepartmental mobility in assistant secretary appointments.

We also recommend that it ought to be open to any assistant secretary who has served at least five years in his/her present post to signal a desire to move, and that a formal policy on mobility should be developed that makes it clear that mobility is encouraged and, indeed, is seen as desirable if an assistant secretary aspires to further promotion.

A greater opening up of senior posts to external competition is desirable. This would be a logical follow-on from the agreement in *Towards 2016* to open a proportion of middle-grade posts to external competition. It would also help to fill skill gaps in specialist areas at senior level. The Australian experience suggests that after such a move most posts will still be filled internally, with the highest posts almost always being filled by internal candidates. Nevertheless, opening senior posts to competition would be an important signal in the drive to create a performance culture.

It remains to be seen whether the levels of remuneration available will be sufficient to attract the calibre of candidate that the Civil Service would wish to attract at a senior level. On the assumption that they are not, then individualised contracts may be necessary. Such contracts are not likely to sit easily alongside the current centrally negotiated pay arrangements and it is likely that a policy will need to be developed on issues such as base remuneration, PRP, tenure and mobility which will apply across departments.

It is recommended that the current bonus system for assistant secretaries be reviewed and, in particular, that the views of serving assistant secretaries be obtained. While PRP systems are likely to remain a feature of the senior Civil Service, the question of extending PRP to other grades should be considered only after the current PMDS system is seen to operate properly, and is shown to deliver credible and clearly differentiated assessments of performance. The use of PMDS assessments for other important reward systems, in particular increments and promotion, is, in any case, likely to be of far greater importance.

In Ireland there is no central, formal mechanism for identifying and developing potential leaders in the public service. In 2002, a subgroup of the SMI Implementation Group of Secretaries General reported on this issue and recommended the establishment of a Senior Executive Service. We believe that the proposals put forward by the subgroup have to be considered again. In particular, we believe that the proposals on establishing candidate groups at Principal Officer level and assessing them against a leadership capability framework – along the lines of the approach in Australia and New Zealand – are essential.

The establishment of an SES should be accompanied by the elaboration of a leadership development strategy for the Irish Civil Service. The creation of a career development assessment centre would be an important mechanism to translate that strategy into specific career development programmes for individual civil servants. The strategy should encompass a policy of mobility for senior civil servants, which would be facilitated by our recommendations in relation to the operation of TLAC.

6

Summary, conclusions and recommendations

Our main purpose in this volume is to identify some key issues to be tackled in the next phase of public service reform in Ireland, and to suggest some practical ways in which this might be done. We have looked at the extensive academic and institutional literature on the recent and ongoing Civil Service reforms in several similar countries, we have visited and met with civil servants involved in this process in Australia and New Zealand, we have considered the commentary from political leaders and other key stakeholders in Ireland, and, critically, we have reflected on our own experience in over a dozen civil and public service organisations in this country.

In examining this material we have concluded, like the Taoiseach and the Secretary to the Government in recent statements, that significant and useful progress has been made over the past ten years in Ireland through the SMI/DBG process but that important tasks remain to be tackled (An Taoiseach, 2006a; McCarthy, 2005). We still lag behind other countries in some key areas of reform. We believe we can usefully look at experience abroad to find pointers for future progress in this country, but that we must be very conscious of the need to root any proposed reforms firmly in the history and current experience of our own Civil Service and its key stakeholders.

Clarifying the key objectives: performance and delivery

In particular we need to be clear about the underlying vision of what we are trying to achieve in the next phase of reform. The Taoiseach (2006b) has recently pointed out that the public service must engage in a process of ongoing renewal in order to 'justify public confidence in its ability to deliver'. There is a similar focus on 'performance' and 'delivery' in comments by many leading political figures both in Ireland and in other countries in recent years. This commentary is normally linked to a recognition of the rapidly changing political, social, economic and technological environment in which public services now operate. This 'permanent white water', as it has been colourfully described, affects all parts of society. In both the public and private sectors, standards of service have risen and the expectations of customers have risen even more rapidly. Among many other changes, new organisational forms have emerged, or become more significant; ICT has continued to widen business possibilities, with the growth of the knowledge economy; and commercial and public service delivery systems have been transformed. In this context the political debate about the role and performance of the Civil Service has also moved on, and at times has become highly critical.

To constantly improve standards of public service delivery in this challenging environment requires improved qualities of agility, flexibility and responsiveness in public service organisations. The ultimate objective of the SMI programme has been to ensure that the Civil Service is capable of delivering the highest possible standard of service to the government and citizens, 'competitive by reference to international comparisons and benchmarks' (*Delivering Better Government*, 1996). This objective remains entirely relevant today. If the next phase of reform is to be clearly focused on this objective it must, in our view, address a number of key areas that are critical to ensuring that the Civil Service is fully responsive to the changing demands placed on it and is capable of meeting, and surpassing, rising service expectations. This will require qualities of agility and flexibility not normally associated with large organisations, but essential to meeting the needs of today. The process of developing and adapting these qualities to ever-changing needs will be continuous rather than once-off.

Three levers of reform: structures, accountability systems and leadership

Many issues will need to be addressed in this ongoing process of renewal and reform. In this volume, we have identified three areas that are of particular relevance to the next phase of reform. We are supported in our view that these issues are critical by a recent OECD review of public service reforms over the past 20 years, which identified six levers of reform covering largely the same areas, and by a review of the reform programme in Australia that did likewise. We do not suggest that the three areas we have chosen are the only important issues to be addressed, or that our proposals amount to a comprehensive reform programme, but we do believe they are essential elements in any programme that is likely to address successfully the challenges we face today.

The three broad areas covered in the report are as follows.

- *Structures* – here the focus is on the attempt to introduce greater flexibility into Civil Service structures, particularly through the establishment of agencies and the use of market mechanisms, and at the same time to ensure coherence and 'joined-up government', recognising that, despite its size and complexity, government remains a single enterprise.
- *Accountability* – a corollary of greater devolution and structural experimentation is an increased focus on how to hold public sector agencies accountable in a way that encourages high performance. This raises profound questions about the relationship of civil servants with the political system, as well as more practical, but important and complex, issues of how best to measure resources used and performance achieved.

- *Leadership* – even with the right structures and account-ability systems, senior managers in the CS will deliver high performance only if they have the required skills and competencies. These need to be defined in the context of the new, more complex and demanding environment, and will not necessarily be the same as those that served the Civil Service well in the past.

These three elements are bound together by the thrust to create the structures, practices and accountability arrangements to let, and indeed make, managers manage for high performance. This is central to the creation of an agile, flexible Civil Service that is focused on performance and achieves high standards of delivery. This is the objective underlying the thinking in this report; we believe it is fully compatible with the vision outlined by the Taoiseach and other political leaders, and also broadly in line with the views expressed by stakeholder groups.

Putting the structures in place: the heavy machinery of reform

The OECD (2005a) describes structural change in the Civil Service as 'the heavy machinery of reform'. It is driven by the need to meet new demands for public services, by political response to public concerns, by decentralisation and specialisation and by the need to develop better arrangements for policy coordination.

The conventional large, Civil Service 'machine bureaucracy' is necessarily constrained in terms of flexibility and responsiveness. The first objective of most structural reform is therefore to free delivery organisations from the constraints of the traditional Civil Service, making them more responsive to customer requirements. Another major objective is to introduce competition into service delivery, making it more efficient. Such reform normally involves the creation of agencies or the use of market mechanisms.

The negative impact of such reform usually lies in the areas of control, coordination and accountability. These can be addressed by way of further structural reform at the centre of the Civil Service, creating new mechanisms and procedures for oversight and coordination.

In common with many other countries Ireland has pursued a substantial 'agencification' programme over the past 20 years, although very few of these agencies are engaged in the delivery of core public services. Most of them were established to deliver specialist services. This has occurred in the absence of any formal framework, leading to a considerable variety of agency types in terms of size, legal basis, operation and accountability, and to inevitable overlap or duplication of functions. There is no formal system of review to assess the performance of, and indeed the continued need for, the agencies. The benefits of this reform are therefore difficult to assess.

We believe that there is a need to bring greater coherence to the roles, operation and governance of agencies in Ireland. This would be facilitated by the following steps.

- Creating a formal framework for the establishment and operation of agencies on the lines proposed by Prospectus (2003) for the health services. The remits of agencies operating within such a framework should be properly focused to take account of whole-of-government objectives.
- Undertaking detailed, formal reviews of performance and continued relevance every five years. This would complement, not replace, ongoing corporate governance arrangements. It would be appropriate when establishing new agencies to set this review process within the context of a 'sunset clause' in the agency service level agreement or memorandum of understanding to underline its significance.
- Developing an appropriate performance indicator framework for each agency linked to the service planning and budgetary processes. The performance measures should also include a whole-of-sector perspective.

The role of departmental officials on agency boards should be reviewed to facilitate policy alignment and agency delivery as recommended by McGauran *et al.* (2005), and the development of departmental capacities to undertake the governance role should be given high priority. Departments with a number of agencies should cooperate in a cross-departmental review to establish best practice. This review should also address the value of establishing separate governance units versus maintaining responsibility within line units.

The relative benefits of creating executive offices within Civil Service departments, rather than arm's-length agencies, merit serious examination. Examples of this form include the Centre for Management and Organisational Development (CMOD) in the Department of Finance and Irish Aid in the Department of Foreign Affairs. While such an office may offer less operational flexibility than an independent agency, there would be fewer problems in aligning policy and it would enable policy-makers to maintain close links to the front line, while separate budget lines from the parent department would facilitate accountability.

The use of market mechanisms to improve performance and delivery is increasing in OECD member countries. There is substantial evidence that these mechanisms can be effective in terms of reduced costs and more efficient delivery of services. However, these do not flow automatically. Mistakes have been made and important lessons learned.

In order to maximise the benefits it is necessary in the first place that there should be a clear policy framework for the use of these mechanisms. Such a framework has been developed for PPPs, and something similar is needed for outsourcing and voucher schemes. However, the value for money of PPPs in large infrastructural projects requires more rigorous, formal appraisal, and their use needs to be kept under review.

Indeed, it is generally desirable that where market mechanisms are used, some public sector capacity is also retained. This is critical in regard to the provision of supervision and governance arrangements. It provides contingency in regard to high-skilled strategic areas and additionally it provides benchmarking and promotes competition.

A primary concern in relation to the use of agencies and market mechanisms for public service delivery is the loss of coherence or of a 'whole-of-government' perspective.

Government policy must be aligned between the centre and the periphery irrespective of what delivery mechanisms are in operation. This requires coordination at all levels in regard to development, implementation and subsequent monitoring.

To enhance this area of performance between departments and agencies, consideration should be given to the introduction of a pre-policy audit process, similar to that pertaining in New Zealand. Regular, structured meetings between all agency chairpersons, CEOs and department heads in a policy area would also be very desirable.

More broadly, we need to consider whether existing mechanisms for overseeing policy implementation and whole-of government coordination are sufficient. The Performance Verification Group and existing cabinet committees may be sufficient to ensure delivery of government policies in certain areas. In more complex situations, and particularly for major new initiatives, we should develop a formal implementation protocol that should itself be subject to central review for effectiveness. Ideally this requires the formation of a Central Implementation Unit, probably in the Department of the Taoiseach, similar to the Australian model.

It is also important that key strategic result areas be identified for each organisation. The relevant implementation monitoring group (PVG, Cabinet Committee or CIU, or C&AG) should establish specific performance indicators to measure collaboration between organisations. These indicators would be chosen to eliminate duplication, discourage territorialism and encourage synergies between organisations. Financial sanctions should apply to defaulters.

Providing accountability for performance

The putting in place of appropriate structures is necessary to facilitate greater agility and responsiveness in the Civil Service, but structures alone will not change behaviour or focus the actions of civil servants on higher levels of performance. Civil servants, like anyone else, respond to incentives, therefore a great deal of attention in reform efforts internationally is being paid to the incentives contained in the accountability systems to which civil servants are subject.

These systems are focused on three broad purposes:

- providing for democratic monitoring and control of public administration
- avoiding misuse or concentration of power and providing assurance of propriety
- encouraging improved performance through reporting on achievements and learning.

In our view, and despite media commentary to the contrary, our existing systems have generally proved effective in the first two of these roles. However, our accountability systems have not been sufficiently focused on performance improvement. They are still more concerned with process than with outcome, and have some important negative side-effects, including acting as disincentives to innovation and risk-taking.

In Ireland, as elsewhere, some changes have been made in recent years to address this, but we can, and should, do much more to ensure that our accountability systems underpin and encourage high performance. In doing so we should observe the five principles for effective accountability identified by the Canadian Auditor General (2002):

- identify clear roles and responsibilities
- ensure clear performance expectations
- provide for the appropriate balance of expectations and capacities
- provide credible and timely reporting
- ensure fair and informed review and feedback on performance and appropriate consequences.

To be meaningful, accountability must be considered with reference to the resources available to achieve performance. Budgeting and accounting practice are therefore key aspects of the accountability framework. This is the thinking that underlies the effort on the management information framework in recent years, and more recently the reform of the estimates process with the introduction of an annual output statement (AOS). It also underpins the much more developed PB systems in Australia, New Zealand, the UK and elsewhere which seek to measure resources used, outputs delivered and outcomes achieved in a more ambitious way than in our current systems.

In Ireland we are heading cautiously towards PB. With the implementation of modern accounts systems in recent years and the work on performance management through the SMI, PMDS and MIF processes, we have in principle already put in place some of the basic building blocks for PB.

We support a move to PB but believe the direction in which we are moving, and its implications, need to be clarified. An effective PB system requires not only new processes, but also changed behaviour by politicians, the Department of Finance and management in line departments. The experience in the countries we have examined indicates that PB must be implemented within a broader framework of devolved control of resources, and a strong focus on results in political debate and administrative oversight systems. The AOS initiative in 2007 and 2008 will provide an important test of whether this is likely to occur in Ireland. It is not yet clear that key players are conscious of the challenge, let alone clear about what they wish to do.

An important technical issue is whether it is desirable to move to accrual budgeting and reporting as part of the development of PB. Accrual accounting can facilitate good financial management and, in particular, can clarify the real cost of projects and programmes. It also avoids some perverse incentives of cash accounting. But the superior information provided by accruals is of little value unless budget holders have real discretion on how budgets are spent, and have the financial knowledge and skills necessary to use accruals information effectively to support their decision-making. Neither of these conditions is currently satisfied in the Irish Civil Service. The following recommendations are therefore made.

- We should embark on a process of recruitment and internal skills development to put in place a significantly enhanced level of accounting expertise. This will facilitate a subsequent move to accruals but is, in any case, necessary in the short term to obtain full value from the modern accounts systems that have been installed.

- We should provide for a greater degree of devolved control within the terms of our current administrative and programme budget systems. Without devolved financial controls there would be little point in moving to accruals.

With these arrangements in place we should adopt accrual budgeting and reporting, as part of a decisive move to PB, once the response to the new AOS has been assessed. If that assessment leads to a decision to adopt a fully-fledged PB framework, with devolved authority and accountability, then the effort and cost involved in a move to accruals will be justified. It is critical that such a decision has strong political backing.

The new AOS/estimates system will pose a significant challenge for the many departments that are not well advanced in the development and monitoring of meaningful performance measurement. If the AOS is to represent a significant step towards a more performance-oriented accountability system, it is vital that the information contained in it is concise, meaningful, and genuinely useful for understanding what is achieved with public funds. The Taoiseach's decision to ask the Implementation Group of SGs to review this information is therefore very welcome. It is recommended that this should grow into a formal system of regular external validation of the performance indicators (PIs) used in the AOS, perhaps by the C&AG. These PIs should be reflected in departments' strategy statements and annual reports, and this validation process would therefore also enhance the useful content of these documents.

Validation of performance information may well become a key role for the C&AG in a future performance-focused accountability system. The work of national audit offices in other countries is also increasingly shifting to performance auditing, augmenting the attest work of such offices. In Ireland the C&AG currently devotes a modest 10 per cent of staff time to value-for-money reports. It is recommended that this be expanded and that particular attention be given to identifying examples of best practice that can be emulated. The current focus of C&AG reports, and PAC hearings, on deficiencies found in the course of the annual audit is a strong incentive to avoid breaches of correct procedure, but does little to encourage high performance. It would therefore be a poor match for a modern, performance-based budgeting and accountability system.

Much of the uncertainty about the significance of the new accountability systems now evolving in this country is a result of a deeper problem about the relationship between ministers and civil servants. Clarification of the role of secretaries general/accounting officers in recent years has been positive but has not been sufficient to deal with the need to define fully the relationships between ministers, SGs and other officials in a way that seems appropriate to the twenty-first century. The Carltona doctrine remains in place but is increasingly questioned by leading figures, including those directly affected by it. An open and well-informed debate between all the key participants is necessary and indeed urgent, but there is currently no space in which to have it. It is essential that this gap be filled, as there is a need to undertake a fundamental review of the relationship between ministers and officials and to define clear and balanced rights, responsibilities and accountability relationships.

Developing leadership capability

Notwithstanding the significant differences between the system in Ireland and that in Australia and New Zealand, there is much that we could learn about the approach and the commitment in those countries to leadership development.

Appropriate structures, and performance-focused accountability systems, are vital components for an adaptive, effective and high-performance Civil Service in the twenty-first century. However, a senior leadership that is capable of using these structures and processes as a springboard to promote performance and delivery seems to us a vital third element.

As the Taoiseach (2006) emphasised recently, when announcing a new leadership initiative for the public service, acquiring this leadership involves more than the development of skills and competencies in the traditional way. The challenge for Ireland centres not so much on trying to decide what kind of leadership the Civil Service needs as on the practical problem of how to acquire it. In particular we believe that getting 'the right people in the right places at the right time', as demanded by the Taoiseach, requires reform of our current systems of recruitment and selection, reward and leadership development.

In common with other countries, we currently face significant challenges in recruiting and retaining future leaders through the normal entry grades. Learning from experience in Australia and elsewhere, a revitalisation of the administrative officer recruitment scheme is necessary to improve the attractiveness of the Civil Service to top graduates. The scheme should be specifically marketed as a top graduate recruitment scheme, with a clear and specific commitment to training and to development through mobility, and with guaranteed promotion, subject to satisfactory service, within five years.

In Ireland, perhaps the key issue, identified by the Taoiseach, is how to ensure that people in senior positions have had a sufficient breadth of experience, across departments and agencies and also across different types of management responsibility. In our view the opening up of middle-level and senior positions to more competition and to outside applicants will help, but it will not necessarily guarantee the kind of leadership the Civil Service needs in the future.

We conclude that a greater opening up of senior posts to external competition is desirable. The Australian experience suggests that such a move will still result in most posts being filled internally, with the highest posts almost always being filled by internal candidates. Nevertheless, opening senior posts to competition would be an important signal in the drive to create a performance culture. It would be a logical follow-on from the agreement in *Towards 2016* to open a proportion of middle-grade posts to external competition. It would also help to fill skill gaps in specialist areas at senior level.

Under our current system, not enough time and effort is put into leadership development and selection. One clear deficiency is the failure to facilitate more mobility in senior grades. We conclude that the following changes are needed in the approach to appointing assistant secretaries and equivalents.

- The practice of the appointing department nominating internal candidates for the TLAC interview should cease, with a view to encouraging more interdepartmental mobility.
- It ought to be open to any assistant secretary who has served at least five years in his/her present post to signal a desire to move. A formal career development policy should be established that makes it clear that mobility is encouraged and, indeed, is seen as desirable if an assistant secretary aspires to further promotion.

Creating appropriate reward mechanisms for good performance in the Civil Service is a challenging task; some research suggests that civil servants tend to value intrinsic rewards, such as feelings of competence and achievement, over extrinsic rewards, such as salary and bonuses. This is perhaps fortunate, as salary levels in senior Civil Service posts have been explicitly set at levels that are not competitive with the private sector. It may also partly explain the lack of enthusiasm for performance-related pay and bonus systems, as evidenced by the failure to implement effectively the current bonus system for assistant secretaries as outlined by the Committee for Performance Awards.

Ireland is not unique in this, and reviews of the experience in other countries with more ambitious systems of performance-related pay (PRP) show considerable scepticism about their direct impact on actual performance. On the other hand, the OECD (2005a) has suggested that PRP can facilitate other organisational changes such as an improved and stronger focus on effective appraisal and goal-setting processes and increased flexibility in work organisation.

It is recommended that the current bonus system for assistant secretaries be reviewed and in particular that the views of serving assistant secretaries be obtained. While PRP systems are likely to remain a feature of the senior Civil Service, the question of extending PRP to other grades should be considered only after the current PMDS system is seen to operate properly. It is only when the PMDS is shown to deliver credible and clearly differentiated assessments of performance that the issue of PRP can seriously arise. In any case, the use of PMDS assessments for other important reward systems, in particular increments and promotion, is likely to be of far greater importance.

In Ireland there is no central, formal mechanism for identifying and developing potential leaders in the Civil Service. The Taoiseach's comments on leadership are only the latest expression of unease at how the current system is operating. In 2002, a subgroup of the SMI Implementation Group of Secretaries General reported on this issue and recommended the establishment of a Senior Executive Service (SES). Features of the SES that the subgroup found would be of value in an Irish context were a systematic approach to developing senior civil servants through:

- challenging assignments
- interdepartmental mobility
- more robust selection procedures
- development programmes and mentoring
- establishment of 'candidate groups'
- external placement
- overseas assignments.

The proposal echoes many of the features of the Australian system, which we had the opportunity to examine.

We concur with the conclusions of the subgroup and would urge the speedy implementation of its recommendations. The establishment of an SES should be accompanied by the elaboration of a leadership development strategy for the Irish Civil Service, and the creation of a career development assessment centre to translate that strategy into specific career development programmes for individual civil servants.

The strategy should encompass a policy of mobility for senior civil servants, which will be facilitated by the measures suggested above in relation to the operation of TLAC.

Concluding remarks

The achievements in recent years through the SMI/DBG process have been considerable, although they are not widely understood by the general public and often not fully recognised even by civil servants. As the Taoiseach (2006a) said recently, 'perhaps we undersell slightly what has been achieved because it has been done over a decade.' However, there is now a palpable sense among our peers in the Civil Service that the SMI process has run out of steam and that the time has come to think anew about the future direction of reform. Recent statements, by the Taoiseach and the Secretary to the Government among others, make it clear that this process has now begun, however tentatively, and that there is a recognition that much more can and should be done to ensure that our Civil Service fully meets the challenges of the twenty-first century and compares with the best in the world in the way that it does so. We think it important that a revitalised process of renewal and reform be directed by a clear strategic vision of where we are headed, and be informed by a realistic but bold appraisal of what is required.

It is in this context that we hope that the views we set out in this volume will prove to be a useful contribution at this time. In undertaking this work we have sought to identify best-practice ideas from the literature or experience abroad, but have also been very conscious that these will only be useful if they make sense and can be applied in the particular circumstances of Ireland. This study is therefore rooted in our understanding of the achievements to date and future requirements of the reform process in this country. The strong desire of the group has been to ensure that the final product of our work is of real use and represents a positive contribution to the ongoing reform process in this country. Hopefully we have succeeded. Like the Secretary to the Government, we believe that 'reform is a challenge worth meeting.'

Bibliography

Aucoin, P. and Heintzman, R. (2000), The dialectics of accountability for performance in public management reform, *International Review of Administrative Sciences*, vol. 66, pp. 45–55.

Auditor General of Canada (2002), *Report to the House of Commons*, Chapter 9, 'Modernizing Accountability in the Public Sector', Ottawa: Auditor General's Office. Accessible at www.oag-bvg.gc.ca

Auditor General of New Zealand (2006), *2005–2006 Report*. Accessible at www.oag.govt.nz

Australian National Audit Office (2004), *Better Practice in Annual Performance Reporting*, Canberra: ANAO. Accessible at www.anao.gov.au

Australian Public Service Commission (2003), *The Australian Experience of Public Sector Reform*, Canberra: APSC.

Australian Public Service Commission (2005), *State of the Service Report 2004/05*, Canberra: APSC.

Bahrami, H. (1992), The emerging flexible organization: Perspectives from Silicon Valley, *California Management Review*, vol. 34, no. 4, pp. 33–51.

Barber, M. (2006), Meeting the demand for improved public services, *McKinsey Quarterly*, October. Accessible at www.mckinseyquarterly.com

Blondal, J. (2005), *The Role of Market Type Mechanisms in the Provision of Public Services*, Bangkok: OECD.

Bovens, M. (2005), *Analysing and Assessing Public Accountability*, paper presented at Accountable Governance: An International Research Colloquium, Queen's University Belfast, 20–22 October 2005.

Boyle, R. (1997a), *Team Based Working*, Committee for Public Management and Research, Discussion Paper 4, Dublin: Institute of Public Administration.

Boyle, R. (1997b) *The Use of Rewards in Civil Service Management*, Committee for Public Management and Research, Discussion Paper 5, Dublin: Institute of Public Administration.

Boyle, R. (1999) *The Management of Cross-Cutting Issues in the Public Service*, Committee for Public Management and Research, Discussion Paper 8, Dublin: Institute of Public Administration.

Boyle, R. (2001), *A Review of Annual Progress Reports*, Committee for Public Management and Research, Discussion Paper 18, Dublin: Institute of Public Administration.

Boyle, R. (2004), *The Role of the Centre in Promoting Civil Service Modernisation*, Committee for Public Management and Research, Discussion Paper 27: Dublin: Institute of Public Administration.

Boyle, R. (2006), *Performance Verification and Public Sector Pay*, Committee for Public Management and Research, Discussion Paper 32, Dublin: Institute of Public Administration.

Boyle, R. and Worth-Butler, M. (1999), *Multi-Stream Structures in the Public Service*, Committee for Public Management and Research, Discussion Paper 9, Dublin: Institute of Public Administration.

Burgess, K., Burton, C. and Parston, G. (2006), *Accountability for Results*, London: HM Treasury.

Cabinet Implementation Unit (2005), Extract from *Annual Report 2004–05*, Canberra: Department of the Prime Minister and Cabinet. Accessible at www.dpmc.gov.au/annual_reports

Carnegie, G.D. (2004), 'Promoting Accountability in Municipalities', *Australian Journal of Public Administration*, vol. 64, no. 3, pp. 78–87.

Chan, M., Nizette, M., La Rance, L., Broughton, C. and Russell, D. (2002), 'Australia', *OECD Journal on Budgeting*, vol. 1, no. 4, pp. 35–69.

Committee for Performance Awards (2005), *Annual Report 2005*. Accessible at www.finance.gov.ie

Committee of Public Accounts (2005), *Second report 2005: Proposals for Alterations in the Way that Estimates for Expenditure are Considered by Dáil Éireann*, Dublin: Houses of the Oireachtas.

Comptroller & Auditor General (2004), *The Grouped Schools Pilot Partnership Project, Report on Value for Money Examination*, Dublin: Office of the C&AG. Accessible at www.audgen.gov.ie

Connecting Government: A Whole-of-government Response to Australia's Priority Challenges (2004), Report for Australian Public Service, Canberra.

Coombs, H.C. (Chairman) (1976), *Report of the Royal Commission on Australian Government Administration*, Canberra: Australian Government Publishing Service.

Co-ordinating Group of Secretaries (1996), *Delivering Better Government: A Programme for Change for the Irish Civil Service*, Dublin: Government of Ireland.

Darwall, R. (2005), *The Reluctant Managers*, London: Reform.

de Coninck-Smith, N. (1991), 'Restructuring for Efficiency in the Public Sector', *McKinsey Quarterly*, vol. 4, pp. 133–50.

Delivering Better Government, Second Report to Government of the Co-ordinating Group of Secretaries (1996), Dublin: Stationery Office.

Department of the Taoiseach (2006), *Irish Civil Service Customer Satisfaction Survey 2006 Report*, Report on Research Conducted for Ipsos MORI, March. Accessible at www.bettergov.ie

Devlin, L. (Chairman) (1969), *Report of the Public Services Organisation Review Group 1966–1969*, Dublin: Government Stationery Office.

Ellis, K. and Mitchell, S. (2002), 'Outcome-Focused Management in the United Kingdom', *OECD Journal on Budgeting*, vol. 1, no. 4, pp. 106–24.

Gould, M. and Campbell, A. (2002), *Designing Effective Organisations: How to Create Structured Networks*, San Francisco: Jossey-Bass.

Fine Gael and Labour (2006), *The Buck Stops Here*, Joint Policy Document. Accessible at www.finegael.ie

Goldsmith Fitzgerald (1999), Staff Retention Survey, on behalf of the Office of the Civil Service and Local Appointments Commission, Dublin.

Greenspan, Alan (2004), Testimony before the House of Representatives Committee on Education and the Workforce, 11 March; quoted in '*A Third Wave of National Reform': The Proposals of the Victorian Premier*, Melbourne: Government of Victoria.

Haran, P. (2003), 'The Irish Civil Service in a Changing World', in *Governance and Policy in Ireland, Essays in Honour of Miriam Hederman O'Brien*, Dublin: IPA.

Hawke, L. (2006), *Department of Finance and Administration: Australia's Experience with Performance Budgeting*, presentation to study group, 18 April.

Herber, J., Singh, J.V. and Useem, M. (2000), 'The Design of New Organisational Forms', in *Wharton on Managing Emerging Technologies*, New York: Wiley.

Hilmer, F. (Chairman) (1993), *National Competition Review*, Canberra: Commonwealth of Australia.

Holmes, J.W. and Wileman T. (1995), *Towards Better Governance – Public Sector Reform in New Zealand (1984–94) and Its Relevance to Canada*. Accessible at www.oag-bvg.gc.ca

Humphreys, P.C., Fleming, S. and O'Donnell, O. (1999), *Improving Public Services in Ireland: A Case-Study Approach*, Committee for Public Management and Research, Discussion Paper 11, Dublin: Institute of Public Administration.

Information Society Commission (2003), *Modernising Public Procurement*, Dublin: Department of the Taoiseach.

Ingraham, P.W. (2001), *Linking Leadership to Performance in Public Organisations*, Paris: OECD.

INTOSAI (2004), *Implementation Guidelines for Performance Auditing – Standards and Guidelines for Performance Auditing based on INTOSAI's Auditing Standards and Practical Experience*, Stockholm: International Organization of Supreme Audit Institutions.

Irish Government Public Private Partnership (PPP) website: www.ppp.gov.ie

Jacques, E. (1990), 'In Praise of Hierarchy', *Harvard Business Review*, Jan./Feb., pp. 127–33.

Kane, A. (1993), *Reforms in Irish Public Financial Procedures: Paper to the Foundation of Fiscal Studies*, Dublin, October.

Kanter, R.M. (1983), *The Change Masters*, Melbourne: Allen & Unwin.

Kanter, R.M. (1990), *When Giants Learn to Dance: Mastering the Challenges of Strategy, Management and Careers in the 1990s*, London: Unwin Hyman.

Kanter, R. (1994), 'Collaborative Advantage: the Art of Alliances', *Harvard Business Review*, July–Aug., pp. 96–108.

Kibblewhite, A. and Ussher, C. (2002), 'Outcome-Focused Management in New Zealand', *OECD Journal on Budgeting*, vol. 1, no. 4, pp. 80–105.

Kristensen, J.K., Groszyk, W.S. and Bühler, B. (2002), 'Outcome-Focused Management and Budgeting', *OECD Journal on Budgeting*, vol. 1, no. 4, pp. 1–29.

Larkin, T.J. and Larkin, S. (1996), 'Reaching and Changing Frontline Employees', *Harvard Business Review*, May–June, pp. 95–104.

Lawton, A. (1999), 'Managing Networks', in A. Rose and A. Lawton (eds), *Public Sector Management*, Chapter 11, Harlow, UK: Financial Times/Prentice Hall.

Leavitt, H. (2003), 'Why Hierarchies Thrive', *Harvard Business Review*, March, pp. 97–102.

Leslie, K. and Tilley, C. (2004), 'Organizing for Effectiveness in the Public Sector', *McKinsey Quarterly*, no. 4, pp. 1–5.

Management Advisory Committee (Australia) (2003), *Performance Management in the Australian Public Service: A Strategic Framework*, revised edition, Phillip, ACT: MAC.

McCarthy, D. (2005), *Public Service Reform in Ireland*, Paper presented to Dublin Economics Workshop, Kenmare, 15 Oct.

McCoy, D. (2006), Presentation to 'Change and Challenges in the Public Sector from SMI to Benchmarking', Public Affairs Conference, May.

McGauran, A.M., Verhoest, K. and Humphreys, P. (2005), *The Corporate Governance of Agencies in Ireland*, Committee for Public Management and Research, Report 6, Dublin: Institute of Public Administration,.

McGinty, B. (2003) IBEC Director's Address to Industrial Relations/Human Resources Conference, Chartered Institute of Personnel and Development, May. Accessible at www.ibec.ie

Matheson, Alex (2006), Personal Communication.

'Meeting the demand for improved public services' (2007), Accessible at www.mckinseyquarterly.com

Minister for Finance, Brian Cowen TD (2005), 'Achieving Value for Money in Public Expenditure', address to the Dublin Chamber of Commerce, October.

Minister for Finance (2006), 'Minute of the Minister for Finance in response to the Second Report for 2005 of the Committee of Public Accounts on Proposals for Alterations in the way that Estimates for expenditure are considered by Dáil Éireann', Circular 10/06, June.

Mintzberg, H. (2003), 'Organization', in J.B. Quinn, H. Mintzberg, R.M. James, J.B. Lampel and S. Ghoshal (eds), *The Strategy Process – Concepts, Contexts and Cases*, New York: Prentice Hall.

Modernising Government (White Paper) (1999). London: The Stationery Office.

Mullarkey, P. (Chairman) (2002), *Report of Working Group on the Accountability of Secretaries General and Accounting Officers*, p. 28, Dublin: Government of Ireland.

Mullins, L.J. (2002), *Management and Organisational Behaviour*, Harlow, UK: FT Prentice Hall.

Murphy, K. (2005) Speech at launch of Democratic Audit by Tasc, June.

National Economic and Social Council (2002), *Achieving Quality Outcomes: The Management of Public Expenditure*, Dublin: NESC.

National Economic and Social Council (2006), *NESC Strategy 2006: People, Productivity and* Purpose, Dublin: NESC. Accessible at www.nesc.ie

New Zealand Office of the Controller and Auditor General (2003), *Key Success Factors for Effective Coordination and Collaboration between Public Sector Agencies*, Wellington, New Zealand: OCAG.

New Zealand State Services Commission (2003), *Working Paper No. 17, Post-NPM Themes in Public Sector Governance*, Wellington, New Zealand: SSC.

Next Steps Report (1988), *Improving Management in Government: The Next Steps*, London: UK Efficiency Unit.

OECD (2001), *Public Sector Leadership for the 21st Century*, Paris: Organization for Economic Cooperation and Development.

OECD (2003), *Public Sector Modernisation: A New Agenda*. Paris: Organization for Economic Cooperation and Development.

OECD (2004), *Public Service Modernisation: Governing for Performance*, Paris: Organization for Economic Cooperation and Development.

OECD (2005a), *Modernising Government: The Way Forward*, Paris: Organization for Economic Cooperation and Development.

OECD (2005b), *Public Service Modernisation: Modernising Accountability and Control*, Paris: Organization for Economic Cooperation and Development.

OECD (2005c), *Public Service Modernisation: The Way Forward*, Paris: Organization for Economic Cooperation and Development.

O'Riordan, J. and Humphreys, P. (2002), *Career Progression in the Irish Civil Service*, Committee for Public Management and Research, Discussion Paper 20, Dublin: Institute of Public Administration.

PA Consulting Group (2002), *Evaluation of the Progress of the Strategic Management Initiative/Delivering Better Government Modernisation Programme*, Dublin: PA Consulting Group.

Peters, B.G. (2006), *Alternative Futures for Public Administration*, Paper delivered at IPA Conference on 'Moving towards the Public Sector of the Future', 8 June, Dublin.

Pettigrew, A.M., Ferlie, E. and McKee, L. (1992), *Shaping Strategic Change*, Chapter 9, London: Sage.

Prime Minister's Delivery Unit (UK), Accessible at www.cabinetoffice.gov.uk/pmdu

Prospectus (consultancy group) for Department of Health and Children (2003), *Audit of Structures and Functions in the Health Services*, Dublin: Government Publications.

Reform (2002), *Spending without Reform: Interim Report of the Commission on Reform of Public Services*, p. 29, London: Reform.

Regulating Better (2004), Government White Paper, Dublin: Government of Ireland.

Review Body on Higher Remuneration in the Public Sector (2000), *Report Number 38 to the Minister for Finance on the Levels of Remuneration Appropriate to Higher Posts in the Public Service.* Accessible at www.reviewbody.gov.ie

Review Body on Higher Remuneration in the Public Sector (2005), *Report Number 40 to the Minister for Finance.* Accessible at www.reviewbody.gov.ie

Review of the Centre (2002), Report of the Advisory Group on the Review of the Centre, Wellington: State Services Commission. Accessible at www.ssc.govt.nz

Rose, A. and Lawton, A. (1999), 'Markets and Bureaucracy', in A. Rose and A. Lawton (eds), *Public Service Management*, Chapter 6, Harlow, UK: Financial Times/Prentice Hall.

Schick, A. (1996), *The Spirit of Reform: Managing the New Zealand State Sector in a Time of Change*, Wellington: State Services Commission.

Schick, A. (1999), *Government of the Future: Getting from Here to There, Opportunity, Strategy, and Tactics in Reforming Public Management*, Paris: OECD.

Schick, A. (2001), *Agencies in Search of Principles*, OECD Global Forum on Governance paper, Paris: OECD.

Schick, A. (2002) 'Does Budgeting Have a Future?', *OECD Journal on Budgeting*, vol. 2, no. 2, pp. 7–48.

Schick, A. (2003) 'The Performing State: Reflection on an Idea Whose Time Has Come but Whose Implementation Has Not', *OECD Journal on Budgeting*, vol. 3, no. 2.

Scott, C.J. (2000), 'Accountability in the Regulatory State', *Journal of Law and Society*, vol. 27, no. 1, pp. 38–60.

Senate Employment, Workplace Relations and Education

Committee, Australia (2005), *Report on Annual Reports*, no. 1 of 2005, Canberra: SCFA.

Senior Leadership and Management Development Strategy Snapshot (2005), Wellington, New Zealand: Leadership Development Centre.

Shackleton, V. (2005), 'Business Leadership', in D. Torrington, L. Hall and S. Taylor, *Human Resource Management*, Harlow, UK: FT Prentice Hall.

Sharman, Lord Sharman of Redlynch (2001), *Holding to Account – The Review of Audit and Accountability for Central Government*, London: HM Treasury.

Shergold, P. (2004), *Plan and Deliver: Avoiding Bureaucratic Hold-up*. Accessible at www.dpmc.gov.au/speeches

Social Partnership Agreement, *Towards 2016*. Accessible at www.taoiseach.gov.ie

State Services Commission [New Zealand] (2005), *Statement of Intent G 3 SOI*. Wellington: SSC.

State Services Commission [New Zealand] (2006), *Career Progression and Development Survey 2005*, Wellington: SSC.

Strategic Management Initiative (2002), *Public Service Modernisation Programme*. Accessible at www.bettergov.ie

An Taoiseach, Bertie Ahern, TD (2006a), *Change and Challenge in the Public Sector – from SMI to Benchmarking*, Speech to Public Affairs Ireland Conference, 25 May.

An Taoiseach, Bertie Ahern, TD (2006b), Opening Address at the Inaugural IPA National Conference, 'Moving Towards the Public Sector of the Future', 8 June. Accessible at www.taoiseach.gov.ie

An Taoiseach, Bertie Ahern, TD (2006c), Speech at the IMI Annual National Management Conference. Accessible at www.taoiseach.gov.ie

An Taoiseach, Bertie Ahern, TD (2006d), *'Towards a New Generation of Partnership: Delivering the Civil Service Change and Modernisation Programme' and Practical Experience*, INTOSAI, Stockholm.

TLAC (1998a), *Report of the Top Level Appointments Committee, 1 January 1984 to 31 December 1997*, Dublin: Department of Finance.

TLAC (1998b), *Guide to Recent Developments, Future Direction and the Procedures of the Top Level Appointments Committee*, Dublin: Department of Finance.

TLAC (2002), *Procedures and Practices*. Accessible at www.finance.gov.ie

Tuohy, B. (2005), *SMI – Ten Years On*, Presentation to Policy Institute, Trinity College Dublin, February.

Turnbull, A. (2005), *Changing Times*, London: The Office of the Civil Service Commissioners.

Uhrig, J. (Chairman) (2003), *Review of Corporate Governance of Statutory Authorities and Office Holders*, Canberra: Commonwealth of Australia.

Vaill, P.B. (1996), *Learning as a Way of Being: Strategies for Survival in a World of Permanent White Water*, San Francisco: Jossey-Bass.

Wall, A. and Martin, G. (2003), 'The Disclosure of Key Performance Indicators in the Public Sector', *Public Management Review*, vol. 5, no. 4, pp. 491–509.

Whelan, P., Arnold, T., Aylward, A., Doyle, M., Lacey, B., Loftus, C., McLoughlin, N., Molloy, E., Payne, J., and Pine, M. (2003), *Cross-Departmental Challenges: A Whole-of-Government Approach for the Twenty-First Century*, Dublin: Institute of Public Administration.

Winstanley, D., Sorabji, D. and Dawson, S. (1995), 'When the Pieces Don't Fit: a Stakeholder Power Matrix to Analyse Public Restructuring', *Public Money and Management*, April–June, pp. 19–26.

Wolf, M. (2006), 'Whitehall Needs a Great Leap Forward', *Financial Times*, 25 May.

Woodhouse, D. (2000), 'The Reconstruction of Constitutional Accountability', *Public Law*, Spring, pp. 73–90.

Appendix:
Authors' current roles
and organisations

Alverez-Antolinez, Carlos – Head of Unit European Commission Food and Veterinary Office

Brennan, Derek – Director of Regimes, Irish Prison Service

McKenna, Louise – Deputy Director, Forensic Science Laboratory

Mullen, Maurice – Assistant Secretary General, Department of Transport

O'Driscoll, Aidan – Assistant Secretary General, Department of Agriculture and Food

O'Reilly, Philip – Assistant Secretary General, Department of Agriculture and Food

Rice, Nacie – Assistant Commissioner, An Gárda Síochána

Sheridan, Michael – Deputy Chief Veterinary Officer, Department of Agriculture and Food

Smyth, Gerry – Director of Audit Office of the Comptroller and Auditor General

Smyth, Tony – Director of Engineering Services, Office of Public Works

Usher, Noel – Director of Primary Care and Social Inclusion, Department of Health and Children

Index